BRING YOUR BUSINESS IDEA TO LIFE
WITHOUT BURNING OUT

JO RICHARDSON

First published in Great Britain by Practical Inspiration Publishing, 2021

© Jo Richardson, 2021

The moral rights of the author have been asserted

ISBN   9781788603010   (print)
         9781788603003   (epub)
         9781788602990   (mobi)

Every effort has been made to trace copyright holders and to obtain their permission for the use of copyright material. The publisher apologizes for any errors or omissions and would be grateful if notified of any corrections that should be incorporated in future reprints or editions of this book.

Cover design by Pressing Buttons
Matches by Vecteezy

 Practical Inspiration
Publishing

Contents

Preface

Ignite was born on a bike ride. I'd been talking to a friend about a sales problem she was facing in her new business and sharing a perspective from my corporate experience. That insight turned out to be the piece she was missing. I realized I had had multiple similar conversations with entrepreneur friends and that was my lightbulb moment! These insights could benefit so many more entrepreneurs and I wanted to make them accessible.

The book took some time to conceptualize. Travelling in Myanmar for the new year in 2019, I woke up in the middle of the night and started to make notes of what my chapter headings might be; the ideas just kept flowing. Another few months passed before I joined a 10 day book proposal challenge online, and after six weeks in a follow-up bootcamp, I had the core structure of my book all mapped out.

By this time the pandemic was in full swing so the book (along with eating too much and not exercising enough...) became my focus, and just six weeks later I had written my first full draft. The pandemic brought into sharp focus the importance of health and wellbeing. Entrepreneurship had always been synonymous with burnout and sacrifice and that needed to change in a post-pandemic world. The need for entrepreneurs to not only balance but prioritize their health and wellbeing alongside their business was now essential and is a core part of *Ignite*.

There are many business books for entrepreneurs, but few that encourage a journey with wellbeing at the core. This book is truly a guide, not a one-time read but a tool that you can come back to as you progress through your business journey.

The online support document, referenced throughout, can be accessed on the author website and provides the reader with a tool they can download and maintain to document their reflections throughout the journey. This content will be useful in informing your business plan and can be used for future pitch work or marketing material for your business. There are helpful reflection exercises throughout the book that can be captured in the tool.

When times get challenging, or you find you are not progressing, the online tool becomes a crutch to help you keep moving forward. Of course, you don't have to use the online tool; however, it's always helpful to capture the insights and revelations you will have along your journey rather than letting them fade away.

Whilst *Ignite* is not intended to signpost specific legal processes or licensing requirements for business set-up, the toolkit and content will take you through a journey to consider the possible areas you need to research and it will direct you in mapping out your approach. It is also important to note that references to 'product' or 'service' are interchangeable throughout so, whether your business is product based or service based, the content and approach is equally applicable. References to clients, customers and consumers should also be considered interchangeable.

There are many references to use of social platforms and networks throughout whose content, purpose and popularity can change quickly so be sure to keep up with changing technology trends as part of your journey. No doubt, in years to come readers may ask what was Facebook?

The landscape may change, but managing your wellbeing should always be a priority. You *can* turn your idea into a reality, you *can* bring that side hustle to life and you *can* do this whilst juggling life and without burning out. It's all in the planning and herein lies your business planning guide.

Don't let your ideas die. *Ignite* the spark and you will see what is possible when you plan mindfully.

Introduction

Entrepreneurship has become a more accessible reality for people over the last decade with the evolution of technology, access to information and the ability to connect on a global scale. Never more so than during the pandemic and post pandemic era was this realized. The world was forced to enhance its digital and virtual capability almost overnight. Large corporates and organizations that would otherwise have taken several years to adjust, were catapulted into their future in a matter of weeks and months.

The shift to conscious consumerism had also been slowly evolving, yet, with the pandemic, this too emerged to the forefront of our minds. A realization occurred that in the face of a global crisis, the material world became irrelevant when our existence was threatened. Health and wellbeing became paramount.

The world was disrupted overnight, yet, despite this meteoric shift into the future, we were paradoxically forced on an individual level to pause, stop and recalibrate. The world had never been so connected and, at the same time, individuals had never been so isolated or physically confined.

This polarization of change brought with it the opportunity for entrepreneurship to disrupt and evolve like never before. People the world over were having to work in a new, agile way, businesses were forced to adapt, mindsets had to shift and we saw an explosion of creative and innovative solutions arising from circumstance.

This global pause created a diversion from the previous cycle of incessant human desire for bigger, better and faster consumption, towards a more thoughtful reflection on what really matters. The answer discerned was almost unanimously health and family. Not only the health of the population, but also the health of the planet and its ability to sustain the incessant and excessive consumption of its host.

So, what does this mean for entrepreneurship? The necessity to adapt brought with it the opportunity to disrupt. The environment has never been more conducive for entrepreneurs to succeed and every industry is ripe for disruption. For those who have dreamed of being entrepreneurs, it is time to stop dreaming and start doing.

Bring your ideas to the world. Find your passion. Be creative. Be innovative. Solve social problems. Utilize technology to enable and globalize your solutions. The world has never needed entrepreneurs so much as during a pandemic and in a post-pandemic world. It is time for you to take the leap, the world needs your ideas and, even if you don't feel ready to explore them right now, then you certainly will by the end of this book.

Reflections

As you progress throughout this book, there are a series of reflection exercises aimed to help you gather and document your thoughts. You can complete the reflection exercises in an online tool that allows you to capture your reflections in one place online (at jorichardson.org). At the end of the book, you will have a neat summary of the key learnings from each chapter to reflect back upon throughout your business journey. Your reflections form a strong foundation for your business plan, and not only capture your current journey through this guide but also allow you to create a document that helps to prepare for future business pitches or customer meetings. Refreshing on these reflections prior to a pitch or customer event, for example, will help keep your messaging consistent and focused.

The reflection exercises will become a practical tool and resource that allow you to quickly refresh on your thinking and approach. You may use your support and feedback reflections, for example, as a quick reminder of where to turn when you need advice and guidance on your journey. When you experience barriers or need to regroup, you can quickly reflect on your purpose and self-limiting beliefs reflections, in order to quickly shift your mindset and approach.

The tool can also be used as a framework for future business ideas that evolve from your start-up. Once you have completed the legwork of reading this book and completing the reflections thoroughly, you will find it easier to use the reflections without having to retrace entire chapters.

If you have taken time to really capture the essence of your learning from each chapter, the reflections will serve as a great 'go-to' tool to refresh on your key focus areas for each stage of the plan. If, on revisiting, you feel your reflections are quite wordy, it is a good exercise to create a more concise version. I would encourage you not to overwrite the previous thoughts and reflections as these may serve well in jogging your memory on your thinking process at the time.

Below are the reflections that you will have worked through by the end of this book. You can document them in whichever way works best for you. The online tool is, however, a great way to have an agile version of your reflections that may be more versatile for future reference and use.

1. Defining your intention – what do I want to do?
2. Defining your long-term goals – what is your moonshot?
3. Defining your values
4. Branding
5. Self-limiting beliefs
6. Defining your purpose – why do I want to do this?
7. Defining your purpose – the consumer lens

1

Intention

What do I want to do?

Clarifying your intention

'Pay attention to the things that you are naturally drawn to.
They are often connected to your path, passion and purpose
in life. Have the courage to follow them.'
– Ruben Chavez

When ideas come, they can be instant flashes of light and
aha! moments that hit us out of the blue. They can also be
slow-burning ideas that, over time, accumulate into a moment
that results in a reflection and realization that everything
that has come before was, in fact, signposting and leading
to this moment. Ideas can arise from moments of despair or
frustration and experiences that we do not wish to repeat
ourselves or for others to experience. Regardless of what has
brought you to this moment, I can assure you that you stand
on the precipice of potential greatness. Whether you explore
that greatness depends on your choices from here on in.

So, you have an idea – what now? Here's where the journey
really begins, and the good news is that this book will help
you through every step of that journey, from ideation to
implementation. The question is: are you ready? The decision
to act, to keep moving forwards and plan with intention is

in your hands at this very moment. Taking small steps every day or week will transform your idea into something real and tangible that others can also see, experience and benefit from.

Let's start by considering your idea. Is it actually the right idea? This may seem like a strange question to pose as you may feel you clearly have your business idea clearly defined and are ready to go. More often than not, however, you will find that as you start the journey, things change. Time well spent honing your idea before action is key. There is nothing more frustrating than being half way down the road and realizing you've actually gone a long way in the wrong direction.

You may have an idea, for example, that you want to start a flower shop to cater for large events. The question is, do you actually need a shop? Could you manage such a business with a distribution channel and an online presence without the need for a shop at all? Depending on whether you see your business being local or scalable will depend on where you begin and whether your idea really is the right idea. Taking time to think this through before starting is critical... it is much harder to change your plans when you are halfway along the journey. Using the online tool, together with this book, will help you easily hone, finesse and expand your idea.

Drilling down into the end goal is important. You wouldn't climb a mountain without first understanding the different routes, what equipment is needed, the time you will have to set aside to prepare and the best conditions in which to undertake the journey. Your business plan is no different. This book will guide you to ensure you're choosing the right mountain to begin with. It will then break down the journey into manageable steps, ensure you have the skills needed or signpost you to where you may need help and expertise.

Let's start by considering and defining the 'what' that sits beneath your idea. Entrepreneurs (you can call yourself that from here on in, by the way) have many reasons for starting a business and this chapter looks at your reasons, your intention and really understanding if that intention is, in fact, your true intention.

Reflection 1: Defining your intention – what do I want to do?

Use this tool to document your idea and clarify it into an intention. This exercise will also help you to sense check that it's the right intention before you move forwards.

List your intention and all the reasons why you want to do this until you run out of ideas. Don't overthink it, just write. When you have run out of ideas just take a few minutes to reflect on what you have written. Start to group your ideas into themes if the list is long. These themes will feed into your motivations in the next chapter. Now, revisit your list and ask the following of each statement.

So that...?

Asking this question will help you to uncover what lies beneath your intention. Again, you can cluster these ideas if it helps or if your list is pretty exhaustive. This exercise and the content you generate will help you later in your journey, informing your branding and marketing content – ideas captured in your toolkit are versatile content so don't throw anything away. There is an example to help you in the online tool, which is also covered here.

Finally, try to draft one statement that concisely captures your intention.

Here's an example to help get you started.

Reflection: What do you want to do?

- I want to write a book to help entrepreneurs turn their ideas into reality.
- I want to make it accessible to any business idea no matter how big or small.
- I want to help people to find the confidence to take the leap.
- I want people to maintain health and wellbeing along the way.
- I want people to see this as a journey that can work to your schedule and timeline even if that takes months or years!
- I want to help readers see the possibility of bringing an idea to life and still fit it into their busy lives.
- I want to ensure that great ideas find their way into the world and not die because they seem unachievable or impossible.

Reflection: so that...

- I can bring my knowledge and experience to others to fast track their journey.
- I can break down the journey into simple steps so that anyone can see it is achievable.
- I can bring wellbeing into the journey and show that entrepreneurs can sustain a healthy balanced approach.
- I can inspire people to take the first step and not let ideas die.

Reflection on themes: Accessible. Simple. Helpful. Manageable. Wellbeing.

Reflection on intention: Have everything in one place for entrepreneurs. Provide equity for all readers of this guide for the entrepreneurial journey. Encourage and foster empowerment. Provide a framework. Focus on wellbeing.

My intention: To write a step-by-step guide for all entrepreneurs to bring their ideas to life and ensure they avoid stress and burnout by focusing on wellbeing throughout their journey. Provide an online tool to document the journey for future use.

People become entrepreneurs for many reasons. It may be to establish a multimillion-dollar business. However, more often than not, this does not begin as the end goal. For many entrepreneurs, starting a business can provide an alternative to the corporate world or the ability to be your own boss; it can be an avenue to balance work and personal demands beyond the 9–5; it can be born out of curiosity and pursuit of a hobby or passion. For some, the desire to overcome social or environmental challenges whilst creating something sustainable is the driving force. For other entrepreneurs, starting a business arises from adversity such as losing a job and seizing an opportunity to pivot into an entirely new career. There are even those who consider starting a new business just for fun. For those in the latter category – proceed with caution – anything worth doing well doesn't often come easily or without challenge.

So, what is driving your intention? What has brought you to this point? It may be a combination of the above; however, I would challenge you that this is not your true intention. This is simply the trigger that has brought you to this point, a trigger that resulted in a decision. Your intention will most likely be bigger and more deep-seated than you realize. Through the next couple of chapters, we will bring clarity to what you want to do, *why* you want to do it and how you will do it or what we will call your intention, your purpose and your approach as an entrepreneur.

As an entrepreneur, it is likely that you may want to just get straight into action; however, clarity and planning are critical to ensuring you are on the right path. The time you invest now in defining your intention, purpose and approach will influence your journey and benefit you further down the line when the journey can become challenging or complicated. When your focus turns to exploring your brand and your networks or your content and client attraction strategies, clarity around your intention, purpose and approach will ensure that you can articulate what you are trying to achieve with stakeholders, clients, customers and investors.

When you have clarity on your intention and you know what you want to achieve at the end of the road, you have identified the finish line. However, you will come to realize throughout this book that the finish line can shift. What you will inevitably find along the way is that your intention evolves, what was once your finish line actually becomes a milestone on a much bigger journey – this is simply growth and the evolution of your business. Let us park this to one side as we have to start this journey before we plan the next! Any ideas that come along the way should not, however, be lost. You can document these in the future part of the toolkit, which can be found on the author webpage.

The future section of the toolkit is a catch-all space, to ensure your creative ideas along the journey are not lost. These future ideas or side roads will no doubt inform your business evolution or expansion. The key is to capture all ideas whilst staying firmly focused on the initial path you have chosen. These future elements may become different paths you explore along your journey; they can be complementary motivations or even secondary business ideas.

The beauty of a business idea is that it can be as big or as small as you choose – it's also yours, which means you get to control the idea or get lost in the idea as much as you desire based on your journey. What's important is that you decide whether to go exploring these paths or stay fixed on your current journey.

Balancing reflection and action

'Follow effective action with quiet reflection. From the quiet reflection will come even more effective action.'
– Peter Drucker

Through the first reflection exercise you have managed to balance both action and reflection. Hopefully, you feel you've achieved some progress already by working through the clarity of your intention and then reflecting more deeply to ensure it is the right path for you and your business idea. This first action and reflection is a small insight into the journey of an entrepreneur and one of the skills required to stay on track. Stepping back to reflect and balance this with action will be a discipline that serves you well.

Throughout your journey, it will become increasingly important to switch between a mountain view and a trail view. Sometimes we can be so focused on putting one foot in front of another that we forget to look up at the mountain top and remember the bigger goal or intention. Balancing reflection and action are critical throughout all the stages of the business cycle. The natural tendency of an entrepreneur is to be in a state of doing so it is important to learn that reflection is essential and is not inaction. Stepping back can sometimes mean that you spot a safer route to the mountain top or you see that other climbers have evolved a technique that is enhancing their journey. You may notice that shortcuts are creating knock on impacts to the terrain making the journey unsafe for others.

When you take a mountain view you can clearly see the full landscape and all the elements in and around your journey. We covered earlier in the chapter how planning with intention is critical. Planning reflection and downtime is also key to your journey and we will explore this in more detail later in the book. It is critical that you build reflective practice into your journey as an entrepreneur. Start to think about your time. How good are you at planning reflection? Can you still the mind and switch off? If not, how might you practise? Hold those thoughts... we will progress to this in Chapter 3 when we explore planning.

Vision

**'If you are working on something exciting that
you really care about, you don't have to be pushed.
The vision will pull you.' – Steve Jobs**

Already, you should be starting to feel some clarity coming together around your intention and your purpose. We have also touched upon the way in which the journey may change as you go along and this is to be expected – growth or redirection are inevitable and you should be prepared for these. We will look at adaptability in more detail in Chapter 2. Nothing in business is certain and the world or economy can change almost overnight. As a business owner, you need to be able to pre-empt or, at the very least, adapt and respond to such changes.

What is important to keep in focus in both good times and challenging times, is your north star – your guiding point. What is your ultimate vision for your business? Whether you are starting small or aiming high, it's important to think about your vision at the outset. If you're not sure where you're going, how will you know you are making progress? We have already discussed how milestones will help with the journey, yet, as those journeys evolve into new ventures or higher climbs, what will be the overarching vision or north star that keeps you focused? You may be starting a small local business but don't let that stop you from dreaming big. Having a vision for your business will help to keep you focused on what you are trying to achieve.

When you reflect back at the intentions exercise, this will provide some of the thinking that may contribute towards your vision but then you should 10× it. What does that mean? Simply that you should enlarge that goal and scale that goal much further than the limit in which it currently sits. Say, for example, you want to set up a local bakery. Why not have the goal of becoming the number one family-owned bakery in your country? If your business is product and sales based, consider it being the number one in a category or geography or even the world!

When you remove limitations and set a moonshot vision, you should feel energized by the possibility and potential. If you believe in your business or your product and you know that the world needs this solution, then why not aim high? Your entrepreneurial spark should ignite when you consider your vision. It may seem bold, it may seem beyond reality right now, but the question should be – why not?

If you set out to write a book, why wouldn't you aim to be a *New York Times* bestseller? The goal may be years away but it should be ambitious. If you establish a bold vision, you will find that your energy, focus and conviction become aligned, enabling you to manifest the end result. There is much content written about the possibilities and success of such goal setting and visualization. Many prominent figures and athletes affirm that through mindfulness, meditation, mental preparation and visualization, they have been able to achieve success and perform at their best. The possibilities for your business are endless, establish a vision without restrictions and limitations allowing your creativity and growth to flourish. Such a vast moonshot goal should be aspirational and exciting as you start this journey.

Reflection 2: Defining your long-term goals – what's your moonshot?

- Think about your original intention.
- Now document some statements that would be a 10× version of that goal.
- What would be the returns either financially, sustainably or based on recognition and reward?
- Would you like your product to be sold in a certain chain or globally used by certain individuals, teams or industries?
- Think limitless and have fun with the statements, no matter how unreal they may seem right now when you write them down.
- Try to bring these statements into one vision. Make this clear crisp and concise. Every word should be relevant. Seek feedback from friends or family on how they interpret your vision and keep shaping or reshaping it until you have something succinct.

You may be starting a local baking business, yet your moonshot might be to be the world number one supplier of healthy vegan cakes. You may be writing your first book and have a moonshot goal of becoming a *New York Times* bestselling author. It may feel like a moonshot and it may take many other milestones to reach there but having that goal will help to drive your focus. Without it, your business may not reach its full potential.

Values

> 'If people believe they share values with a company, they will stand loyal to the brand.' – Howard Schultz

Having a clear intention, purpose, vision and values will help to guide you and also your employees if your business expands and you decide to hire a team around you. These core elements will also define the way that you operate within the business, how you make decisions and how you engage with your client. When times are tough, these elements will also provide an anchor to keep you focused on what you always set out to achieve. Even when your business is challenged, a strong purpose, values and vision should help steer you back onto the right path.

In the same way that you have so far established clarity around your intention, purpose and vision, this should also filter down into your values. Your business values will inform many decisions along your journey, they will define the culture of your team or organization; they will inform the journey that your customer experiences, and they will inspire others to buy into your brand as an employee or investor. People buy people, and it is the values that radiate from those individuals and their teams that they align with and commit to.

You will no doubt have experienced times when you have voted with your feet when a brand or service let you down and didn't deliver what it said, and what you believed, it would do. The consumer has this choice and your values will ensure that you and your teams align with the consumer to make decisions that build your brand strength and following. The more clarity you have around your values, the more clearly this will enable you to communicate with your clients and these values should be close to your heart. You should be passionate to your core that these values are what your business is about. Even if challenged by a customer or investor – if you have taken the time to define these correctly you will be able to stand by them and deliver on them for your consumer.

Is this necessary, you may ask? You may be feeling that your small local business has no need for values. You have your intention and your purpose. You are clear on what you want to do and why you want to do it. These are your personal guiding points whilst your business remains small; however, they may also be a guide for others as your business grows. Your business exists outside of you and others may need these goals verbalized to understand the direction of the organization. The clearer your vision and values, the better your employees will be able to make day-to-day decisions or offer ideas aligned to these.

As an entrepreneur, you will no doubt feel inextricably intertwined with your business in the initial stages; however, as your business grows, your role within that business will inevitably change. You may not always be the sole driving force. You may employ teams or even sell the business. Those around you need to understand the *what* and the *why* of the business independently of you as a person or owner in order to sustain its success. The intention and purpose of the business in isolation from you as the entrepreneur are established through the vision and values.

The vision and values will be a guiding point not only for those within the business but also your consumer. Through your vision and values, you will start to build your brand. Your intention and purpose will undoubtedly inform the vision and values; however, they will also create an identity for your business that can be viewed independently of you as the entrepreneur or business owner.

Establishing your vision and values at this stage will help to guide you through some of your branding and marketing decisions in the coming chapters. Having these concepts firmly documented should help you to feel as though you are bringing more clarity to your idea and starting to see it take shape as a future business. Your consumer or client begins to take centre stage and you realize that your idea is dependent on many external forces not simply your own energy, passion and drive. Being connected to your consumer and the right consumer for your business or product is achieved in part from your values and vision.

Now is another important point at which to take a mountain view. In setting your values, it is important to go back to your intention, purpose and vision. Scan the horizon. Is the consumer ready for this idea or product? Do you see them needing something specific from your product or service? Is there a changing trend in the market place or environment that could impact your values? A quick scan and sense check is helpful throughout your business planning. If you are creating a sustainable business, what are the trends around sourcing, packaging or production methods? If you are creating a food product, what are the trends around health and nutrition? Do you see a new trend on the horizon that can be considered at the outset? Is your product something unique and high end where quality is critical but the consumer also expects a 'green' product?

Reflection 3: Defining your values

- Take some time to consider brands that you are loyal to.
- Choose one and research what the company vision and values are.
- How do you see this translate into the product or service they provide?
- How have they scanned the horizon in recent years to pre-empt or adapt to a change in consumer need?
- Now consider your business. You have your moonshot vision.
- What are the values that will need to sit under that vision in order to deliver it?
- Keep these succinct and limited in number.
- Try not to have more than three.
- An example may be a business whose vision is to be the customers first choice for x (x being their product or service). Their values may be:

> Do the Right Thing, Better Together and Never Settle.
> - These simple three values are enough to guide their employees to make the right decisions and take the right actions in everything they do.

Brand

**'Your brand is what other people say about
you when you're not in the room.' – Jeff Bezos**

Less than one chapter into this guide and you already have clarity on your intention, purpose, values and vision. That's great! Take a minute to congratulate yourself on the journey so far. It feels good, doesn't it? So, what's next? It may feel strange to have thought about your business outside of yourself when you went through the exercise on vision and values. Although your business is a clear extension of you, it must start to form its own identity. Your product or service must clearly be felt and experienced by the consumer. In its own right. This is your brand.

Many people are advocates of Apple products because of the solutions it provides and the service they experience as a consumer. They did not set out buying into Steve Jobs the person; the product speaks for itself. Hence the evolution of Apple and its products under the new leadership. In a strange paradox, as an entrepreneur, you need to balance your own brand and the brand identity of your business idea. The two can co-exist but at this early stage would not operate in isolation.

Your personal brand is a collection of perceptions. The perceptions others form of you are based on what they see, hear or experience, and sometimes not directly but through what others say about you. Your physical appearance, online presence and the way you communicate in various forums will collectively contribute to your brand. How others then speak about you will also create another level to your brand in the form of advocates or detractors.

In the early stages of entrepreneurship, your brand is pivotal in ensuring you are accessible to as relevant and broad a consumer base as possible. If your brand is associated with negative connotations, you can risk losing an entire consumer segment. In a world that is hyper-connected, a brand can expand exponentially through online forums and sharing of content by so-called influencers. Equally, a brand can be destroyed almost overnight. You will have seen many big brands making errors in marketing or production that have left them exposed. Some brands recover from these incidents and become morally conscious as a result. Others simply fail to come back from these disasters and subsequently follow a steady downward spiral. So brand is important! The strength of your brand will grow your customer base in good times and help to retain it when things are not going so well.

Reflection 4: Branding

- Think about a brand you admire. What do you like about them?
- How does this translate into their product, service and packaging?
- Think about the person that represents that brand or the multiple faces that represent the brand.
- What do they have in common with each other?
- What do they have in common with the brand itself?
- How does their personal brand and the product brand align?
- Now consider your brand – how would people describe you and your brand?
- What do you stand for?

- Is your personal brand strong enough or do you need to better define and communicate it to others?
- Now consider your business brand – what are the words you want consumers to use when describing your business brand or product?
- Are there strong connections between your personal brand and your business brand or is there work to do on bridging the gaps?
- Try to filter your personal brand and your business brand to three words each. Your business may represent equality, integrity and choice, for example. Ensure that the words really mean something to you personally and to your brand.
- The strength of your brand will help to attract and retain clients, so be clear about the brand you are building.

As you begin to establish your business identity through your vision and values, think about the words and language you will use when talking about your company. Take some time to write these down. These words and phrases will become a source of content for future marketing or speaking events about your business or even part of your pitch for investment. Is your business about sustainability, ethics, quality, accessibility, etc.? Think about your consumer. What is the consumer need that your business will resolve?… even if they don't know they need it yet.

What is your unique selling point (USP)? If you're starting a flower shop or cake business, how is it any different to the one in the next town? If you have a product idea or innovation, what will make it unique? Are you able to patent it? What does your business do for the consumer that others cannot or have not thought of? How have you scanned the horizon to pre-empt consumer trends and changes? An entrepreneur with foresight is a powerful combination.

When considering your brand and USP, it is important to focus clearly on the consumer not the competition. Looking left or right may mean that you miss what sits right in front of you. It's not too soon to start your homework and activity around building and publicizing your personal and business brand.

Limiting beliefs

> 'The only thing that's keeping you from getting what you want is the story you keep telling yourself.'
> – Tony Robbins

This guide promises to bring a reflective element to your entrepreneurial journey and a mindful approach to your business planning and execution. You have become accustomed in this chapter to pausing, reflecting and taking a mountain view before carrying on along the entrepreneurial trail. Before we move on to look at motivation and mind in Chapter 2, let's take a moment to consider the reflections so far. No doubt, they have not all been plain sailing. As you have paused and questioned your purpose and intention, there may have been doubts that have crept in along the way. That inner voice that raises questions you don't want to hear. The inner critic that conflicts with your entrepreneurial spirit. Whilst you may have been able to put these thoughts aside temporarily to progress through the exercises it is important to call out those thoughts early on and explore them.

If you start off on a mountain climb thinking that you can't complete certain parts of the climb or are less capable of using some equipment in your toolkit than other experienced climbers, these doubts will become magnified when you are actually faced with them. Your climb will be pursued in a half-hearted manner, with hesitation and anticipation of failure along the way. This underlying doubt will manifest itself into reality, often subconsciously. Dealing with self-limiting beliefs at the outset of your journey will help you identify and overcome some of the challenges ahead.

Beliefs can be positive and powerful or negative and destructive. We will have all experienced times of self-confidence and feeling invincible and also those moments of despair and recession. Fortunately, you have the power to control your beliefs and you decide how they manifest. With practice, planning and exploration you can reframe your limiting beliefs, enabling you to reposition your thinking in order to overcome them. Exploring your limiting beliefs at the outset will ensure that they do not raise their heads unexpectedly and derail your journey further down the line.

So, what is a self-limiting belief? Before you started this book, you probably had moments where you thought 'I can't start a business because'… and your list of excuses far outweighed your motivations. When you reach a tipping point and your desire to progress is stronger than your list of excuses, thus begins your journey to growth. That doesn't mean to say the journey is easy and doesn't require serious discipline and commitment. The motivation will get you started and when times get tough it is the discipline you build around it that will keep you going. As you progress and start to see the results, the motivation comes back into play and will drive you towards the next stage on your journey.

Spend some time exploring your self-limiting beliefs in the reflection exercise. Once you have a list of these limiting beliefs focus on turning them into positive statements. For example 'I don't have time' becomes 'I have the same 24 hours in a day as everyone else'. 'I can better plan my time to make this a priority', 'I can schedule 1 hour a day', etc. You will soon realize you have solutions for most of the self-limiting beliefs you hold. 'I don't know how to run a business' becomes 'I can understand how to run a business through researching and speaking to people who are already doing this'. 'I'm no good with numbers' becomes 'I can do basic maths and I can find an expert to learn from as I go for more complex problems'. The entrepreneurial mindset needs to be one that can easily adapt to a solution mindset. If you struggle to disable your self-limiting beliefs, your entrepreneurial journey will be much more challenging and you will be susceptible to burnout.

Take time to complete this exercise fully and notice how you feel as you're writing the beliefs and how you feel as you transform them into positive statements. The shift from negative and destructive limiting beliefs to powerful and positive statements is empowering for the mind. This exercise allows you to surface those underlying doubts and address them directly with your own positive reinforcement. By coming up with solutions and possibilities you remove the negative power they hold over your subconscious. This is a great practice to use whenever doubt creeps in throughout your business journey. The good news is you don't always have to find the answers and undergo this journey alone. We will explore how to leverage your networks and support system effectively in Chapter 4.

Reflection 5: Self-limiting beliefs

Take some time to list your self-limiting beliefs as an entrepreneur.

They may be beliefs such as:
- I don't have the time/ money/ resources to start a business.
- I don't know how to run a business / I don't know how to set up a website, etc.
- I don't have what it takes to succeed… the willpower… the qualifications… experience
- I could never do x…
- I don't have the skills to do x…
- Who will listen to me I'm just x…
- I'm just one person I can't change or impact x…

Turn those into positive statements or actions and notice how you feel when you read them now.

As we near the end of this chapter, reflect back on your activities and business plan and you will see that with just a few reflections and some commitment, you have already moved your idea closer towards a reality. You have a clear intention, purpose, vision and values, and some clarity about your personal brand and that of your business. You have also started to remove those seeds of doubt that may have been holding you back – that's a lot of progress in just one chapter don't you think? Well done!

No matter how long the journey takes, as long as you keep moving forwards you are making progress towards your business taking shape. The mountain climb is not a sprint. It is a steady advancement day by day. A step forward each day or week is progress in setting up your business, the only thing that will slow you down is when you stagnate. You have reflected on what this business really means to you, you have identified your intention, your 'what'. Let's not stop there. It's time to take this further and clarify your purpose – your 'why?'.

2

Motivation and mind

Why do I want to do this?

Passion and purpose: finding the why?

'Purpose directs passion and passion ignites purpose.'
– Rhonda Britten

At this stage, you will have a clearly defined intention from the first chapter and the reflection exercise. You have defined what you want to do. In this chapter, we will explore *why* you want to start your business. This will be your purpose. Why is this idea so important? What are the real drivers? What motivates you about bringing this idea to life? It is important to explore your motivations and ensure they are going to benefit you and your journey in a positive way. Motivations can arise for many reasons and have much deeper seated origins and value than we realize. Exploring these motivations will help to provide further clarity around your initial intention and will also inform your purpose.

As we explored in the first chapter, your intention informs your brand, your vision and your values. If your business is going to scale up, this also translates into your company culture and how you hire talent into your business. Clarity on your purpose is equally important. Your motivations will ground and focus you as you learn and grow through your entrepreneurial journey. It is critical to document your motivations and your purpose early on in order to reflect back and remember why you started, particularly when times get challenging. It is inevitable that you will grow and change as the business evolves; remembering the real purpose of why you started will help to anchor some of your future business decisions. Without documenting your purpose you may reflect back with a different lens and not recall the real purpose you had at the outset. During this chapter you can use the online tool to help define your purpose.

Clarifying your motivation and purpose at this stage in your journey will also be a firm foundation for when we come to explore what success looks like in Chapter 7. Your motivations will help to define and shape the outputs and measures of success. What does the finish line look like? What are the milestones along the way? Why is this important? Remember the trail view and the mountain view. If you don't stop to look up as you climb, you miss the amazing view and the opportunity to recognize, enjoy or even celebrate your progress. As a business owner, you will become caught up in action and constantly thinking about what comes next. As we mentioned in the first chapter – taking time to reflect on the journey is also important.

It is therefore critical to document and capture your purpose. When times are tough or you cannot see the mountain top because you are experiencing bumpy terrain underfoot, you will need to rely on these motivations to see you through. During this journey you will be balancing your mountain and trail view perpetually, and it is precisely when you are balancing reflection and action that these documented motivations will keep you on track. Your motivations have to have strong, deep-rooted foundations. These are your purpose, your reason for being an entrepreneur.

It is worth exploring briefly here the synchronicity between purpose and passion. Passion is an emotion – it is a desire or enthusiasm for something whether conceptual or material but it is not the object or concept itself. Purpose is focused – it is the action, the output or result of passion. It is what you do in the moment because of how you feel – it is not driven by longer-term focus.

You may climb the mountain in awe of the nature, and excited by the journey ahead you are absorbed in each moment and the experiences and emotions – this is passion. But when the fog and the cold set in, and you are tired and hungry, the passion quickly subsides. That is when your purpose takes over. You are climbing this mountain for a reason and when passion subsides it is your purpose that will keep you going. Passion will help you to enjoy the journey but purpose will keep you focused on getting there.

Let's start exploring and defining your purpose. You will notice that as you start to explore your purpose, passion will creep in. That's the joy of reflecting, it allows you to discover yourself along the way. As you continually sharpen the focus away from your passion the purpose becomes clear. In the same way that we defined *intention* or the 'what' in Chapter 1 we will now define the *purpose* or the 'why' in this chapter.

Define your true purpose by completing the reflection activity and keep questioning what sits behind each statement. What are you trying to enable by your statements?… In order to do what…? Draw out the one overarching purpose that sits across all your ideas. You may have many reasons for your journey and your motivations may lead you down many paths in the future. Being clear on your overriding purpose will ensure that whichever path you go down you are maintaining the same sense of direction – your purpose.

Reflection 6: Defining your purpose – why do I want to do this?

You may find it helpful to revert back to your first reflection where you identified your intention. Your initial reflection may have been more customer-focused statements and solutions. Consider here what are the personal motivations. What's in it for you?

- I want to provide customers with... in order to...
- I want to improve x with my product in order to...
- Consider more emotive words and outcomes and feelings.

You may want to make a million dollars but why? In order to... provide for my family? To ensure the best education for my children? In order to ensure my family health can be protected? To be able to reinvest the money in x charity? To reduce the suffering caused by x?

Take time to really reflect on how you want to feel and what you want to experience as a result of achieving your goals. Reflection takes time. The purpose here is to really search deeply as to what sits behind the surface motivations.

Now that you have defined your purpose, we will spend some time reflecting on it a little further. In sense checking that nothing has been overlooked, you also begin to build your own discipline and practice of getting comfortable with stopping to take a mountain view, ensuring you are not hooked on the adrenalin of the action or business idea alone. The key to this book is not to race through to the end with a half-baked plan and get going. The key to a robust plan is to think it through, understand the journey and what the pitfalls could be and have some tools in place before you begin that will get you through. This is not to say your plan will be 100%

robust for all scenarios as no one has a crystal ball; however, it will make a bumpy journey a lot easier to get through and provide you with skills and disciplines that will enable you to react, respond, innovate or adapt along the way.

Mindful motivations

> 'Choosing purpose over profit can be the most profitable thing you'll ever do.' – John Sanei

Entrepreneurs are born out of a diverse range of circumstances. You may start your business in order to give back to a community, or to help create a sustainable business, you may want to share your knowledge or inspire others. Your business idea could be an invention or you may simply want to sell a product or an idea and make millions. We will now start to explore a little further what you initially defined in your purpose and what sits behind this.

Take some time to look back at the words and phrases that you listed when redefining your passion and purpose. Were you using emotive words to describe your purpose – were you focused on helping others or wanting to make others feel a certain way? Was your language action based and focused on delivering a set result or financial goal? Was your purpose the act of stopping or preventing existing ways of being, such as an environmental issues or animal welfare?

You may notice that your words can have a negative or positive energy to them. If your business idea is born out of wanting to stop or prevent something you feel strongly against this is absolutely legitimate however, you may want to turn that into a more positive purpose. If your business idea is about closing down a competitor it comes with an aggressive and negative undertone. Think about how you can rephrase that into a positive idea. Could you work with that competitor to enhance your idea? Could the businesses actually be complementary in some way? Could you identify a USP (unique selling point) that would move you away from being focused on them to being focused on you? Who cares you may ask? Again, a moment for a mountain view reflection.

If your business idea originated from what you perceive to be a setback or a knock-back, it is important to deal with this personally before you start your new venture. If you do not take time to unpack these events and understand how they impacted you and your emotions you can be certain it will raise its head further down your business journey in unwanted and unhelpful ways.

When you are able to reposition challenges you may have faced on your journey as events that are simply redirecting you, you can master your inner voice to see adversity as opportunity. If this is not addressed from the outset, the inner self talk will creep in later down the line – doubts and tough times will give rise to barriers and bad business decisions.

Approaching and developing your business with the right mindset is critical and that is why an entire chapter is dedicated to this part of the journey. It is important to create solutions from a place of calm not chaos. If you recognize chaos as a potential starting point for your business, take time aside to reflect and unpack this before you move further on the journey and avoid making subconsciously chaotic decisions. Always start your business from a place of peace and positivity, not war. Reposition and pivot the experience or emotion into a positive fresh beginning rather than focusing on a competitor or responding to a string of events that have impacted you negatively.

If you are motivated by competition, what will be your motivation when that company pivots into something else or dissolves? What will your employees focus on and be guided by? Your motivation should be intrinsic and offer solutions to the extrinsic. Even if your idea is born out of a challenge frame it in a positive way. Rather than set up a gluten-free business out of frustration at the lack of choice, pivot that initial idea into educating others on gluten-free alternatives and how to create tasty and gluten-free options for all. We continually see fast food chains partnering with health food providers or plant-based products to offer something for everyone rather than going head-to-head as rivals.

If your intentions are positive, this will be clear in your vision, values and brand. You will attract the right consumer who will easily align and buy into your business. You also need to consider what the consumer may be thinking in one or two years' time and try to cater for future trends even if the consumer hasn't explicitly indicated that intention yet. Consider recent attitudes towards plastic. These shifts and trends have been on the horizon for some time, yet it is only in light of recent movements and the focus on individuals who have brought this to the attention of world leaders, that the awareness turned into a social shift of intolerance towards plastic straws and the utilization of single-use plastic such as water bottles.

The conscious consumer

'Every time you spend money, you're casting a vote
for the kind of world you want.' – Anna Lappe

Your business success relies solely on one thing, your consumer. Whether that consumer is one big tech giant who you need to buy your product or a million online users of your product, one thing's for sure, without them you don't have a business. Broadly understanding your consumers before you begin is, therefore, critical. You need them. You need their support, their respect, their commitment and undoubtedly their time and money. Everything you explored in the first chapter considering your mission, brand, values and intention will either bring consumer loyalty or detractors. Always remember, your consumer has choices. Even if your product seems unique, a replica or alternative is never far away. What will keep your customer loyal when a cheaper alternative is produced?

In 2020 the shift towards conscious consumerism became more focused than ever. The global pandemic pressed pause on the world as we knew it and we were forced to stop, slow down and appreciate what was really important in life. When the material world was no longer easily accessible, we began to realize that health, not wealth, is king. We began to see the impact our lives were having on the planet and on humanity. Whilst many people spent that period craving the return of the old way of life, there was a clear shift towards an enlightenment that things needed to change. The idea of conscious consumerism became more evident and widespread. Large corporations started to shift towards a focus on green, sustainable projects. Governments talked more about carbon neutrality and green energy – coincidence? No – but an acknowledgement of the shift in consumer focus.

So how does this fit with your personal motivations for starting a business? Your motivations may be short term and small scale initially but who knows where this business may be going? Start small but continue to dream big. Maintain the balance between action and reflection, the trail and the mountain. The more you can see the synergies between your own motivations and those of your consumer, the more concrete your brand, values, mission and purpose will become. Consumers will buy into your brand long before your business ideas have even become a reality. We touched upon this in the branding section of Chapter 1 and will return to this when we look at marketing in Chapter 4. This is another crossroad where passion and purpose combine. Your purpose that you clearly defined in Chapter 2 will attract or even push you to cross paths with those who are passionate about the same beliefs and aspirations. Your business may become a vehicle for them on their own journey of growth.

Whether your business is a local start-up or potential global enterprise, you should consider the long-term impacts of your business as you begin your venture. Sustainability, ethical trading and the environment are at the forefront of the consumer's mind and they should be firmly embedded in your business plan. Your future consumers are emerging from a more conscious generation, whose principles are rooted in altruism. If you are starting a business that relies heavily on plastic or operates with disregard for the environment, you will be diminishing your potential consumer pool before you start. Technology is also a huge influence on business. This is a subject that deserves an entirely independent consideration, which this book does not permit; however, be sure to scan the horizon for technologies impacting your field. We will touch on this briefly in Chapter 3.

Conscious consumers clearly see the link between their decisions or individual actions and the cumulative global impact. In a highly connected world, consumers are more aware than ever that they are not isolated in their thinking and one person can start a ripple that reaches millions of consumers. This should not deter an entrepreneur from venturing into business. On the contrary, this connectivity provides an opportunity to listen, align, influence and expand like never before and should of itself be one of the motivating factors that brings excitement to your entrepreneurial spirit.

Reflection 7: Defining your purpose – the consumer lens

- Take a minute to reflect back on the exercise where you defined your purpose.
- Did you consider the consumer?
- Do you need to reflect again on this exercise from a consumer perspective?

- Is there something you missed out that needs to be considered and captured now?
- Think again about your business and note down some of the areas within your business where you can see sustainable, environmental or ethical opportunities.
- These reflections will help build consumer confidence with your brand.

Motivation and discipline

> 'Discipline is choosing between what you want now and what you want most.' – Abraham Lincoln

We have touched upon passion, purpose, motivation and consumer alignment so far and it is important to question the so what of all this. As we take a moment to reflect back on the journey so far, you should start to see some clear links and threads appearing from your initial intention through to your purpose and the consumer needs. Remembering these clear alignments when business becomes tough will help you to remember why you started. Sometimes you will need the voice of someone else to remind you or the support of others to join those dots when they seem broken.

There will be times when you are near the summit and cannot seem to find the energy, motivation or point of getting to the top anymore and it's easy to give up rather than push through. Take time to remember why you started, and reflect on your intention way back when your business was just an idea. At one point your conviction was so strong that you decided to quit one path and follow a tougher mountain climb – starting your own business.

When you are no longer able to connect with the emotions that drove you to this point these reflections will be a reminder of why you started. By the end of this book, you will have a series of reflections that not only outline your business plan in one place, but also serve as a tool that you can return to when times are tough to remind you why you started. Discipline around your routines and practices will guide you when motivation is lost. When the passion subsides, the purpose kicks in. When the trail underneath is bumpy, focus on the goal – the mountain top – and just keep going. Forget the climbers ahead of you. Forget those who seem to be passing you effortlessly or you may lose your footing. Focus on your journey – one step at a time.

Adaptability

'Every success story is a tale of constant adaptation, revision and change.' – Richard Branson

So far, we have spent much time anchoring your business to a clear path. We have identified the mountain to climb, why we are climbing it and how we will get there. We have assessed what tools we have to hand and how we will manage some of the subconscious doubts and limiting beliefs we hold about our ability. All these steps have been important and relevant. You have a robust plan. However, this doesn't mean to say that your plan is rigid. Equally, this is not to say that everything you planned for before is lost. Sometimes you need to shift your climb to a different mountain face altogether.

As you begin and continue on your business journey, it is critical to stop and scan the horizon for changes. Whilst the timing of the pandemic in 2020 was not predictable, its inevitability was. The likelihood of a global pandemic had been foretold by many. Stopping to take a mountain view and considering these changes and challenges throughout your business lifecycle is critical. Scanning the horizon results in preparedness and opportunity – particularly if you notice things that others do not yet see.

Your focus should always be your consumer. Staying one step ahead of their needs rather than focusing on your competitor actions is pivotal to business success. Consumer needs are constantly changing and technology is ever evolving. Your ability to adapt quickly to these changes will help to future-proof your business. If you start your business assuming it will look and operate in a certain way in five years' time, you may be in for a shock or worse if you are not aligned to changing technologies and consumer needs.

Being adaptable is also not tantamount to responsiveness or reaction. Adaptability needs to be within the DNA of your people, leaders and processes. You can build adaptability into your business plans from the outset. In the same way that the climber packs and prepares for a climb anticipating change, you can build adaptability into your plans and mindset. This is a necessary approach for an entrepreneur. Few entrepreneurs are successful in their first attempt at business yet their constant ability to adapt, reshape, learn and grow sets them up for their 'overnight' success. Those who remain fixed on a goal or intention that does not move with the times or align with its consumers are destined for demise.

The pandemic that started in 2020 resulted in significant pivots for many global brands. Airbnb, whose main business model is connecting home owners and short-term lets across the world, localized its entire model to connect people to local longer-term lettings for lockdown as people shifted away from cities towards more rural spaces. Their expansion plans halted and they pivoted towards a new online offering of 'Experiences' – a diverse range of intimate virtual activities from tarot reading to horse whispering! Quite a shift from letting holiday homes!

Whilst your business may only experience a crisis once in its lifetime, such a crisis could signal the end of your business unless you are quick to adapt and innovate. The Covid-19 pandemic saw a range of businesses utilize their existing platforms and production plants to provide support during the pandemic. Health products were made in factories previously manufacturing car parts, large distribution networks were used to move protective equipment and alcohol production was replaced with ethanol production for hand sanitizer. Businesses around the world quickly pivoted and partnered in the crisis. Airlines, despite being hard hit by the drop in commercial travel, were able to sustain some level of operation through critical supplies of cargo.

Many businesses were slow to react and waited for the end of the pandemic. When that end did not come quickly enough, many business soon faced bankruptcy. Such crises are difficult, almost impossible to anticipate. As a business owner or entrepreneur, you can simply be ready to adapt. Take a step back and think about what the consumer really needs in that moment. What are their main priorities? Can you leverage your current business model to produce a much needed product? Can you partner with others to utilize your supply chain and online sales platform to sell an entirely different product in this period? If you're offering a service, can you take it online?

If you need some food for thought as to how businesses have changed and pivoted in recent years consider these. Uber – the world's largest taxi service – doesn't own taxis. The largest accommodation provider, Airbnb, doesn't own real estate and the world's largest movie house – Netflix – owns no cinemas. Your business can be an enabler in times of crisis. Ensure you can step back from what is happening to the business you started and think about the business your consumer needs. Shifting your mindset in times of change is critical to the survival of your business and we will explore this in the next section.

Reflection 8: Adaptability

- What ways have you seen your industry disrupted in recent years?
- How will technology disrupt the future of your industry?
- What are some of the key trends and shifts in consumer habits?
- How adaptable is your business model – consider your supplier contracts and speed to market?
- What well-established parts of your business could be leveraged in a crisis – point of sale, supply chain, production space?

Mastering your mind

> 'Failure is so important. We speak about success all the time but it is the ability to resist or use failure that often leads to greater success.' – J. K. Rowling

Success is rarely achieved without the solid foundation of failure and subsequent learning and growth. Whilst many thought leaders have come to develop an aversion for any words with a negative connotation, the word failure need not be bilaterally opposed to success. They are, in fact, two necessary parts of a spectrum. Success does not exist in isolation of failure. In fact, without failure you cannot have success. Setting semantics aside, there are few, if any, entrepreneurs who will claim to have achieved success on their first attempt.

The journey of an entrepreneur is a challenging one. The very essence of entrepreneurship suggests that you are developing something new and it would therefore be logical that experimentation and learning would be part of that journey. There will be challenges and barriers and unexpected outcomes despite considered inputs. The growth lies in how you overcome such challenges, how you learn from them and how you are able to bounce back from the experience quickly and in such a way that continued challenges can be perceived as redirection and sending you on the right path. The journey won't be easy but with the right mindset it can be endured more easily.

Mindset

> **'Once your mindset changes, everything on the outside will change along with it.' – Steve Maraboli**

What exactly is mindset? The concept of mindset was popularized by Carole Dweck in a book of the same title, where Dweck established the links between mindset, potential and growth in a model that explores two mindset types – the growth mindset and the fixed mindset. In brief, those with a fixed mindset believe that qualities are fixed and unchangeable, whereas those with a growth mindset believe that abilities can be developed and strengthened through practice. Where you sit on this spectrum will have a significant impact on what you feel is within your gift to influence and change in life. As an entrepreneur it is likely that you will have a natural tendency towards a growth mindset, as you are already in the space of creatively thinking of something new and unknown, and venturing into something that you may not have the full skill or knowledge to take on. Or it may be that you assume in your mindset you don't have that capacity.

Your mindset is impacted and influenced by many external factors including society, politics, religion and education, to name but a few. Over time, a shift in all of these areas to a less conservative and more democratic free and equal approach in many, but not all, pockets of the world has led to a conscious awakening of the potential we have as individuals. The idea of reaching your potential and that potential having limitless possibilities opens up a world of opportunity for growth.

So why is mindset important for an entrepreneur? We discussed earlier in the book how your intention and purpose will help to guide you through a tricky climb. They will help to remind you why you started and anchor you in focusing on the end goal if you get side-tracked or delayed. So far we have focused only on the possible barriers being external factors, barriers that come in the form of environmental changes or competitor impact.

The entrepreneurial journey is not only impacted by the external environment, we also have the more complex and often subconscious internal environment to contend with – the mind. To add a further layer of complexity, the mind is already hard wired with almost automatic responses and seemingly logical reasoning based on years of experience and layers of behaviour patterns formed from birth. Some patterns even precede that point and are primitive instincts such as the response of fight or flight.

The purpose of this chapter is not to get side-tracked with psychological theory. It is important, however, to understand some simple triggers, responses, behaviours, patterns, and thoughts or limiting beliefs that you may hold. Without some level of understanding or awareness of these elements, it is likely that you will make poor decisions, endure a much slower learning curve and possibly repeat mistakes along this entrepreneurial journey.

We talked about unpacking some of the potentially unhealthy or self-limiting beliefs that you may hold in Chapter 1. Taking time to identify, unpack and process negative thoughts and turn them into a more positive motivation to succeed is a critical starting point in understanding the importance of mindset. If the reflection and rephrasing of those thoughts was new to you, it may have taken time to work through and taken some real introspection and challenge. It would be easy to dismiss those thoughts and move on without unpacking them and reframing them, yet we know they would have reared their heads further down the line.

The purpose of this book is to enable a balanced, considered and mindful approach to your entrepreneurial journey. This almost goes against the grain for the gung-ho, fast-thinking, fast-paced creative mind and spirit of the entrepreneur where fail fast and move on wins the day. There is, however, a more mindful and considered, and conscious approach. Being a mindful entrepreneur does not mean the journey is slower or less entrepreneurial in spirit, it is simply well thought through and planned out, taking a continual mountain view rather than racing along the trail at lightning speed, failing, falling and rushing on ahead regardless.

The external environment is largely out of your control as an entrepreneur and will undoubtedly influence the internal response; however, what is within your control is the ability to control that response and the shape it takes. This can only be achieved through practice and consciously creating new patterns and ways of being that enable new responses and outcomes.

We will work through a reframing exercise on this shortly. Consider a recent example of when you faced a challenge or setback. Some examples may be from a recent incident in the workplace, in relationships, in sport or even as a parent. Think for a moment of your instant response to that scenario. What were the physical, mental and emotional manifestations of that response? How quickly did they arise and how long did they last? How much did you feel in control of those responses? Now translate those into your business journey. What would be the long-term impact of responding this way to each setback? How would it impact you? How might it impact those you work alongside or those you live with? How might your relationships be impacted?

It is clear that our mindset and our ability to respond in a considered way can have wide-reaching implications not only on our own physical, mental and emotional wellbeing but also on those around us.

Let's take the simplest of examples that most readers could relate to. Suppose you are on your journey and as you walk the trail you stub your toe or trip and fall. A simple yet largely universal experience for analysing your stimulus-response! There is a split-second between the incident happening and the physical response. Undoubtedly, some people's reaction times may be quicker in limiting the impact of the fall, or their muscle memory may provide the balance and reaction to prevent a full fall – these premises are based on the brain's layered pattern around previous such incidents. The mental and emotional processing of the response is, however, fractionally slower.

You may find you curse almost instantly but this is a response you have learned and allowed to embed because you have trained your brain to do so. You have wired your brain to respond in this way, or worse, it may even escalate that rage into a secondary aggressive response such as kicking the offending object away in anger. The emotional response of the impact of the injury, the element of despair that your journey has not run smoothly and the subsequent mental reflections begin processing. These reflections and emotional responses lead to further physical changes such as the body physically contracting into surrender through sunken shoulders or deep sighs, all under the weight of this small stumble on the path.

If we have wired our brains in such a way that those thoughts are allowed to magnify, they become overwhelming negative reinforcements. We may find ourselves going so far as to question why we are even doing this mountain walk and coming on this journey in the first place. What's the point? If we hadn't gone on this journey in the first place, this fall could have been avoided altogether. How quickly the mind can shift from focusing on climbing to a mountain peak full of ambition and purpose and intention to quitting altogether over a simple stubbed toe.

This is just one small, relatable example of how our mind can escalate the smallest of setbacks into a debilitating outcome of surrender in a matter of seconds or minutes. Let us translate that concept for a moment into your business journey. You will appreciate the importance and power that mastering your mindset can have. It is not something to be overlooked and could, in fact, be the difference between success, failure, recovery and progress.

The mind is equally capable of producing a more productive, positive, growth-orientated outcome with the exact speed and response rate to the exact same scenario. You have the ability to program your stimulus response. Between stimulus and response lies choice. It exists within a split second on the time continuum but can be manipulated with focus and practice. The more you focus on this choice and identify the moment where it begins you can start to program how it ends and the outcome or response.

I recently programmed myself to respond to such stimuli by laughing. This response was the antithesis of a previously learned pattern to such a scenario. The more you practise this response, you begin to notice that it becomes more automated and subconscious. The time between the stimuli and response shortens to the point where it becomes the new response. You have effectively reprogrammed your brain to respond in a newly defined way.

Learning new behaviour and having the ability to recognize, control and change your response to stimuli or triggers can be game changing. As an entrepreneur, leader, parent or partner, this mastery of the mind and practice of mindfulness can change your perspective and approach entirely.

Reflection 9: Reprogram your response

Think of a recent example of when you became frustrated because you could not do something or something didn't go your way.

- What was the situation?
- How quick was the emotional response?
- What benefit did your response bring to the situation?

How could you have responded differently that would've added value either to you as an observer or to the other person (if your example involved someone else)?

What could be the new programmed response that would benefit you?

It could be as simple as breathing and closing your eyes for a few seconds – anything that allows you to break the previous learned stimulus response that was holding you back or negatively impacting the future.

Consciously practise the new response over the coming weeks and notice the difference in your physical and emotional state as a result.

Mindfulness

> 'Rather than being your thoughts and emotions,
> be the awareness behind them.' – Eckhart Tolle

Entrepreneurship and mindfulness may not be two things one would think can go hand in hand. The idea of fast-paced, action-orientated entrepreneurs seems at odds with the concept of mindfulness. Yet, throughout this book, you will come to learn that reflection is not inaction. Mindfulness does not necessarily equate to stillness – at least not physically. Being present in the moment and practising mindfulness can, in fact, spark innovation and creativity.

If you recall the first chapter of this book, we talked about how ideas come to light. Those aha! moments. More often than not, these ideas come seemingly out of the blue, yet it is often because we are being present or mindful that the idea is allowed to surface from the chaos of an otherwise busy mind. The mind receives over 10 million bits of data per second and the conscious brain has to filter this in order to processes 50 bits of information per second. It fights to identify what matters, what is familiar and known, what it can leave to subconscious default or a stimulus response that is learned. In being mindful, we become more aware of that processing and can start to slow down and focus in on the information we want to see and process rather than what the mind chooses to do seemingly automatically as our main computer program.

As an entrepreneur, it is important as you progress along your journey to plan time to reflect on the past but also spend time being present and mindful. In the midst of the chaos and frantic schedule of starting, promoting and growing a business it is important to have times where you also allow the mind to clear and allow clarity to ensue.

Now might be a good time to explore briefly why this matters. Why is mindfulness and a growth mindset so important to the journey for the entrepreneur. Surely, it's equally valid to take an active approach and crack on with the journey, just get going and deal with the obstacles and issues as they arise, battle through them in whichever way is needed and keep striving to that mountain top. Yes, this is possible, but the journey doesn't have to be this way. You will no doubt have heard countless stories from entrepreneurs who have experienced burnout, depression and significant detrimental impacts to their health, wellbeing and personal relationships. You want your business to be a success, but defining and planning that success so that it does not come at all costs is critical.

If you find that you have established a successful business but your relationships, health and wellbeing have all been sacrificed along the way, there will be little that a million-dollar deal can do to repair the damage. The mindful entrepreneur can plan their journey to ensure that the things that matter are not jeopardized along the way. The things that matter may change and as long as they are positive changes towards growth then this can only be a good thing. When the values that you held dear in the initial stages of planning are replaced by material goals and a disregard for sustainability, you will certainly lose your most important partner in your business – your clients.

We will explore this a little further in the next chapter as we unpack how, when and where you undertake your entrepreneurial journey.

Optimal performance: body and mind

> 'You have to expect things of yourself
> before you can do them.' – Michael Jordan

There are so many factors that contribute towards optimal performance. Consider some of the world's top sprinters. Every single element of their preparation time is planned out to ensure optimum performance – from nutrition and sleep to mindset and recovery. The athletes' performance is about incremental gains not only in their event but also everything preceding and following it. The athlete invests more time off the field ensuring that their body is able to perform than actually performing itself.

Athletes need to ensure their nutrition maximizes energy outputs. They will take time to ensure robust recovery utilizing sleep for muscle repair in addition to procedures such as cryo technologies. Even their mind has to be trained to cut out external distractions and visualize winning. All this effort is placed in preparation for the main event, which could last as little as nine seconds.

Your business performance is equally important and, whilst you may not need to be in athletic condition, you do need to ensure your daily routines enable you to deliver your best performance over sustained periods of time. The tale of entrepreneurial burnout is all too well known but can be avoided. We have already discussed mindset and physical health is equally as important as mental health. I'm not talking reaching peak physical fitness in addition to setting up a business; however, balance is important.

You may find that you combine your mindfulness with exercise. Mediation and mindfulness need not be inactive states. You may find you can practise mindfulness through yoga, running, swimming or walking. In fact, any activity where you can switch off from the outside noise and focus on the present moment, particularly when it is a routine or repetitive task, allows you to become more present. When the mind is able to switch off and perform these tasks more mindfully, this is often when ideas and creativity can come.

We will explore how to better plan and control your time to allow for this investment in balancing your physical and mental wellbeing in the next chapter. After all, success at all costs is not the goal.

Manifesting

'Whatever you hold in your mind on a consistent basis is exactly what you will experience in life.' – Tony Robbins

We explored briefly in Chapter 1 idea of establishing affirmations from your self-limiting beliefs. This reflection was an introduction to the importance of mindset and to becoming more aware of the inner voice. The more you spend time practising meditation and mindfulness, the more aware you will become of this inner voice and whether it plays a positive or limiting role for the most part. When an athlete is at the starting line they are not questioning whether the person next to them is faster or had more sleep last night or is using a better nutritional plan. There are no questions of what if? There is no doubt at that point. There is only self-belief. They will be reinforcing to the mind that they can, it is possible, this is their race!

What is important as an entrepreneur and business owner is to notice when the negative is creeping in and how to silence it. Before the inner voice even starts to talk, there is a physical reaction in the body. It can be as obvious as a sigh, or a change in body posture. If you can notice the physical triggers, you will be able to silence the inner voice before it even speaks.

For every physical trigger, practise being able to counteract with a positive affirmation. If something has gone wrong that initial sinking in your body posture should be the trigger for a positive affirmation such as – 'this wasn't meant to be so I must be being signposted to a better solution'. Start to notice your physical triggers and prepare some positive redirection and affirmations. In time, they will become automated responses to the physical without the need for you to consciously apply them.

The same approach can be used to address any crisis of confidence that you may experience as an entrepreneur.

There will be times when you're due to pitch your product or maybe present your business offering at an event. Treat this moment like an athlete. You can stand at the office door with sweaty hands or you can tell yourself in the weeks and minutes leading up to the moment that you can do this. Your product is great. What you offer as a service is best in class. All of these positive affirmations should be to hand in your mind ready to pull out at the first sign of a physical trigger. You will often see reporters ask athletes before an event – are you nervous? They will say they are excited or another positive affirmation. They have spent months and years training their mind to interpret the physical triggers as positive indicators. They don't have butterflies, they have excitement. They aren't scared, they're ready to push out of their comfort zone. Their mindset is fully focused on a positive interpretation of the physical reactions.

When the inner voice is allowed to take over, you may experience imposter syndrome. A belief so debilitating that it can prevent many great ideas from coming to life. Doubting your skill and ability to do great things may mean never taking that first step towards entrepreneurship. By the end of this book, you will have the tools to keep imposter syndrome at bay and bring your ideas to fruition. There will be challenges along the way; however, as you reflect through each chapter you will become more equipped to adapt and respond to challenges with the right approach allowing you to quickly move on. The only thing that differentiates us as humans is the choices we make. We are all born with the same potential and so few of us realize it during our lifetime.

3

Planning and focus

How, where and when?

The how?

Managing time

> 'The key is not to prioritise what's on your schedule,
> but to schedule your priorities.' – Stephen Covey

We have spent considerable time in the first two chapters focusing on your intention and purpose. Through the reflection exercises you will have found some clarity around motivation and mindset, managing your perspective between a trail and mountain view and establishing some robust values that will inform your brand and vision. Now that the focus is clear, it is time for action. But wait, how are you going to fit all of this in?

We each have a level playing field when it comes to time. Many things are not equal in life, but we all have the same 24 hours in a day. Our choices through life will no doubt have determined our circumstance; however, what we do with the next 24 hours is yet to be determined. You may have a full-time job or multiple jobs, you may be a busy parent, you may be a carer or you may be spending your free time socializing, volunteering or playing sports, so when will you have time to be an entrepreneur? This thought alone is where many of the aha! moments and great ideas burn out and get lost forever in the despair of the time continuum.

Reminding yourself that we each have 24 hours is very grounding. When you look at your role models – people you admire and are inspired by or even those throughout history who achieved great things – they all had the same time as you to do those things. The only difference is in the choices you make. Many times, you will read about the sacrifices you have to make. However, this word has a far too negative a connotation.

If you have found your passion, if you are truly inspired to do something that will change your life or change the world, you have to adapt. You have to form new habits, make new commitments to yourself and others, and be disciplined in your focus to achieve your new goal. Do not see this as a sacrifice; see this as growth. You are moving towards new goals, new habits and a new way of being. You are becoming your future self and discovering new ways in which to shape your life and spend your time. Undoubtedly, others around you may be impacted by this and feel this change too, and they may grow and adapt alongside you.

This won't always be the case and, as you progress along your journey, you will find that your friends may change, your social groups will shift, you will find yourself surrounded by like-minded individuals and people who inspire you further on your journey and with your goal. This new path and focus will be complemented by others on the same journey.

Let's return to our mountain climb analogy. When you announce your intention to make the climb, you will undoubtedly receive varied reactions. There will be those who are cautious and remind you of the dangers, and there will be those who scoff and ask why? There will also be those who encourage and may even want to join in the journey.

When the climb becomes reality, it may well be that some of your inspired friends start to drop off from the idea of the climb when they realize it involves a lot of training or an investment in equipment. There will be others who you feel less inspired to engage with as your focus and conversation is about the climb, and you feel that those common threads you once had have now shifted.

This is growth. This is you progressing on your journey, following your passion and igniting your spark. Whilst you may feel some sorrow as friends slip away and the journey becomes more lonely, you have to know that there are others who share your new passion and purpose who will go along the journey either with you or as loud voices of encouragement behind you. You cannot spend time mourning your future memories – all the things that could, would or should have been with those friends. You have to forge a new future with new people, embracing the new, not wandering in the past.

We will discuss support networks later in the book. Let us return to the concept of time. As an entrepreneur, you may find yourself in any range of scenarios. You may have left full-time employment to put your all into this new idea. You may have a full-time role and be cautious about taking the plunge and are, therefore, balancing the risk by creating your business as a side hustle. You may be a full-time parent juggling family responsibilities and wondering where you could possibly find the time to start a business. As with all the previous chapters of this book, the key is planning.

You may feel that your day is already full and you cannot possibly move any of your commitments. If that is the case, then you may have to chip into that sleep time. I say this with a caveat that you also need to ensure this is not to the detriment to your health and wellbeing. No one does great work on two or three hours of sleep without an impact to their health. Throughout this book, the focus is on becoming an entrepreneur in a mindful, healthy way. It doesn't have to be about 22 hours of work, exhaustion and success at all costs.

It is important to take some time and reflect on your day and how you approach time. Are you a planner? If you're not a natural planner, it's time to start breaking your day into smaller chunks of activity in order to see how your time is spent. How productive is your time? Do you have a lot of leisure time? Is there time in your diary that can be used more efficiently or effectively such as during a commute or downtime? Most of us are guilty of having those Netflix or TV binges – imagine what you could do with all that time accumulated over a week. How many hours could you find from your current busy schedule? Are there things in your diary that you do from habit that actually don't add value to your future self? It may be time to renegotiate your schedule. Humans have a huge propensity to adapt, and with focus and discipline you can achieve great things.

Reflection 10: Maximize your time

Take time to look at your typical week – if you don't plan it currently, start to plan out where you spend your time.

- What tasks do you do that add value to your goals?
- Where do you spend time that doesn't enhance your growth?
- What are some of the non-negotiable tasks – work, etc.?
- What opportunities are there to share some tasks, e.g. school runs, chores, business activities – leverage your support groups to create time.
- What can you stop doing – what are some of the bad habits that you can cut down or cut out?

- Where can you use time more effectively, e.g. commuting, breaks, downtimes?
- Where can you multitask – can you read and walk or listen to content whilst doing chores?

Knowing your energies

> 'Your energy is currency. Spend it well. Invest it wisely.'
> – Unknown

When considering how we spend our time, it is also pivotal to know how our energy patterns shift throughout the day or week. As you reflect back on the previous exercise and you review your time, you may notice that you have a tendency to do certain activities at certain times of the day because this suits your energy levels better. You may also notice that when you're not productive, you are going against the grain of your energy. Exercising is a simple example of how to consider your energy levels. If you wake up full of energy it's likely you will have your best workouts first thing in the morning. If you find it takes time to wake up and your energy improves throughout the day, you may be best suited to evening workouts.

The same consideration should be given to your mental activities throughout the day when looking to optimize your performance, effectiveness and creativity. Find your power hours! If you are managing your day job alongside a start-up, granted you may not be in full control of your diary at work; however, increasingly organizations are shifting to a more empowered and flexible way of working. Utilizing these opportunities to master your time and energy can be game changing.

If you are more productive and high energy in the morning, are you scheduling the right workload at this time? You will tend to be at your most passionate, creative and inspiring at this time – how are you capitalizing on this energy for your own benefit and those of others to see? Whether that's hosting team sessions or being a creative parent and playing games, taking children out for exercise and fresh air or blocking your time with key stakeholders for your current or future business. Know your energies and play to them.

If you find you tail off towards the afternoon – this may be a time when you can schedule the more mundane tasks that are obligatory in work or at home. When energy levels are low, perform tasks that require less creativity and are more repetitive or almost subconscious. This is the time for those chores that just have to get done whether it's at home or in the office – the tick box, must-do activities that we all have to work through. Then comes the evening.

Consider your downtime. How are your energy levels in the evening? Are you slowly winding down? Are you a night owl and just starting to come alive and feel energized? Are you less productive in the last few hours of the day. Is this simply based on habit? Could this be an opportunity or a window where you could fit in some time to focus on business?

There will always be habits that can be broken and segments of time that can be better spent. The key is to find those golden hours and create new habits around them. Taking this step back to analyse your time is another mountain view moment. If you blindly rush into starting your climb or business venture without having thought through how you can perform at your best and utilize your time most effectively, you may end up with a great business as an outcome but the sacrifices and cost may not be outweighed by the sense of achievement.

The goal of this book is to equip you with some tools to help you achieve your goals whilst balancing your wellbeing and time. You will form new healthier habits, move close to your goals, balance your priorities and all in the same 24 hours you had before.

Balancing mind and motion

'I've learned that you can't have everything and do everything at the same time.' – Oprah Winfrey

When you have identified your power hours and the times when you do your best work, you can align the relevant business activities to your schedule. Being an entrepreneur is not all fun, creativity and passion. Anything worth doing takes hard work, commitment, some setbacks and many twists and turns along the way. We explored previously how the passion subsides on the mountain climb when things get tough and that's when your purpose kicks in. You have to remember why you started. What is your goal? Why did you begin this journey? We previously touched upon the importance of mindset and the need to stop, pause and reflect to consider the journey so far and the journey ahead. There are also times when you need to pause and reflect to recalibrate internally – both physically and mentally.

When you press pause you will find yourself at a crossroads on the journey. There will be times when you feel you have the option to keep pushing forwards or simply pause and take a break. We must remember that this reflection is not inaction. Even inactivity is not inaction. Physical inactivity and stepping back from a strict routine can bring the one thing that you need most – perspective.

There are times when we simply need to stop, pause and rest. You may have a great plan, a robust schedule, a clear alignment of your energies and know how to maximize your time. Yet, sometimes, your brain or body are simply exhausted and need to stop. The mind and the body are constantly working to deliver the demands you put on it; however, it isn't a machine. It requires inactivity and calm in perfect balance to action and processing of information.

Fortunately, the human body has a great way of telling you when it's time to rest and we are all aware of these tell-tale signs before illness kicks in. The key is to practise and embed the mindfulness we explored in the previous chapters in order to prevent this burnout and exhaustion – all too familiar problems experienced by entrepreneurs.

If we return to our analogy of the mountain climb, whilst the journey lessens simply by putting one foot in front of another, stopping to rest and gain perspective and analyse the journey so far and the journey ahead can be sufficient in reigniting the passion and focus. Your business is no different. Sometimes taking a break and switching off can be when ideas and creativity just come. If you remember your original aha moment, it was most likely happening not when you were thinking hard for a solution or idea but when your mind was freely processing or resting. Sometimes rest days are the days when everything comes together.

Meditation and mindfulness

> 'Stillness is where creativity and solutions
> to problems are found.' – Eckhart Tolle

When you finally recognize the need to pause and reflect or simply to rest, it's important that you do so with a positive intention. We previously explored mindset and the importance of reinforcing your actions and decisions in a positive way. When you recognize the need to pause and reflect, it is important that your self-talk is focused on why you have stopped. You are giving yourself time to reflect and come up with new ideas. You are allowing your creative energy levels to refuel and allowing your brain some downtime from working so hard in the previous weeks or days. You are creating space for more ideas and allowing your body and mind to re-energize for what will come next.

This positive reflection is far more productive than allowing yourself to spiral into a negative spin where you may find your inner voice whispering that stopping is failure; inaction is not progression. Stopping to rest is a weakness and you cannot do this. You're failing if you're not moving forwards. Do not allow those negative thoughts to creep in. Remember why you started this journey. Think of this moment of pause as recalibration time, the stillness before the next burst of action, the moment when you should stop on your mountain climb and admire the view and the journey so far. Take pleasure and pride in how far you have come rather than dwelling on what remains ahead.

It's easy to say these things and much harder to put into practice. The journey of a conscious entrepreneur is to bring these practices and disciplines into your routines. The more frequent these practices become within your schedule, the less time you will need to spend recalibrating over long periods of time. Try to identify time in your schedule that allows for meditation. If this can be practised weekly or even daily, you will find that you become more aware of your thoughts and in time will be able to master and control your inner voice and quickly silence the inner critic.

The great thing about mediation is it can be explored with just ten minutes of your time. We are all guilty of spending time flicking through social media; watching TV or consuming content online that adds no value to our growth journey. The practice of applying 'airplane mode' not only to your phone but to your personal life is a great way of creating that space to focus. Placing a virtual 'do not disturb' sign over a set period of time and creating boundaries for thinking space can generate some amazing outcomes. Unfortunately, it takes more effort than the slide of a button.

Simply by replacing this time with the practice of meditation is a great start to controlling your inner voice and creating clarity surrounding your goals and intentions for the day. When we consider meditation, many of us think of sitting cross-legged in a quiet place and trying to stop all our thoughts – impossible in your busy schedule as a parent, employee or an entrepreneur who has to make money today or who knows what tomorrow will bring? Right? Wrong!

It is worthwhile briefly exploring the difference between meditation and mindfulness. Whilst closely interlinked, meditation is best understood as a practice that is undertaken in a set period of time whereas mindfulness is a quality or state of being in which one can exist constantly. Both suggest an element of doing and being, yet are often undertaken with a level of awareness that is considered, conscious and calm.

Meditation can be seen as a practice that nurtures mindfulness; however, it is not the only path. Mindfulness is, after all, in its simplest form, awareness. Being in the present moment, suspending any judgement, engaging fully in the here and now.

In a world that is fast paced and ever-changing, taking time for stillness and to be present brings with it many benefits. We spend our time looking down at technologies in our hands – so much that we forget to look up and see what is in front of us. Meditation is the practice of stopping to look up for just a few moments from the chaos of the world.

There are varied methods of practising meditation and time does not permit an exploration here. Suffice to say, that for any busy entrepreneur juggling life's challenges, building in meditation as a practice will enable focus, concentration and clarity whilst reducing stress and anxiety – all critical for a successful and conscious entrepreneur to master.

The where?

Creative space

> 'Having a clear mind and a clear space allows
> you to think and act with purpose.' – Erika Oppenheimer

Now that you are clear on your intentions and motivations, and have clearly mapped out how you will stay focused and have a robust schedule that balances action and reflection, it's time to check that you have the correct environment in which to operate. You may not have given this much thought yet; after all, some of the great entrepreneurs have built million dollar businesses from their basements, garages and spare rooms so what does it matter? Well, space is important. The moments when you have your creativity in flow and you are working on some great new ideas can so easily be lost in a split second of a doorbell ringing, children coming into the room or a barista cleaning the table next door – so choose wisely.

If we reflect back to the earlier section, this links closely to the idea of knowing your energies. There, we considered *when* you do your best work in terms of time. Here, we look at the environment around you, and *where* you are at your best. Some people find they are at their most creative when they have some background noise whilst others need near silence and peace.

Taking time to think about your working or thinking space and creating that environment is important. Once you have identified the space, protecting that space is even more critical.

What's important to remember here are the basics. What are the key basic things you need to work most effectively and create a space where you have those basics? If you manage to find anything above those basics then that's a bonus. So, what are your basic needs?

Depending on your business, you may need very different things for your creative space or business. If your business is largely centred on creating online content, then you will certainly need somewhere you can sit comfortably and possibly for long periods of time with good Wi-Fi! If your business is based on production, you may need a large space where you can create or experiment; maybe you need a kitchen for parts of your creative time or a space where you can move around if your product is fitness related. Whatever your business idea, take some time to think about the space you might need when creating. If you need outdoor space – just think about how that plays out in various weather conditions!

It's important here to note the difference between space to evolve your business idea and the space you may need when going live with your idea. It may be that you need two very different spaces at different times. Your creative time may be spent at a desk putting together your plans; however, you may then need a kitchen, lab, studio or premises for the actual business to start. Maybe your product will transition from being manageable in a small space to needing premises as things take off. It's worth considering all these elements at the outset to really understand what you might need and when.

Most entrepreneurs tend to start businesses in their own homes and, as production increases and their product overtakes their house space, it's a sure sign that things are going well and it may be time to consider a new model for your production. You may be concerned about the cost of space and premises, and it's important not to jump into this expense too soon. The right space can easily be carved out of your current living space or a public or shared space without any additional cost. If you feel unable to utilize space at home, then shared space is a great way to find temporary space without long-term commitment.

The typical life cycle of a business shifts from start-up to growth, expansion and innovation or diversification and then maybe collaboration or sale. Along the way, there may also be pivoting or downsizing as the environment changes. When considering the potential life cycle of your business, ensure you have identified space where you can quickly flex and pivot as needed without incurring significant costs. Take some time now to research briefly if the space you need is easily available near you.

One of the benefits that emerged from the pandemic in 2020 was a shift towards more flexible working space. Large businesses found they did not need people to travel into cities and central spaces, which led to a reshaping of the workplace and a flexible approach to shared space – a great benefit to many start-ups who do not need or want long-term and sizeable commitments. If you are managing your business start-up as a side hustle, you may be able to attend your office earlier or stay later to work on your side hustle – provided, of course, there is no conflict of interest and the relevant parties agree to this.

So, we have identified two types of space – a location for thinking and a location for doing. They may be one and the same or two different locations altogether. Take some time to think about what works for you.

Reflection 11: Creating the right environment

- What are some of the basics you need?
- Does the space you have in mind cater for all of these?
- What may be some of the barriers ?
- Can you overcome these?
- What are the pros and cons of different spaces, e.g. accessible, opening hours, travel time?

- Is there an alternative space, solution or shared space – think of all the possible opportunities – consider friends' homes, family, leisure spaces, coffee shops, libraries, shared office space.
- Can you organize to stay on in the office after hours or before hours if you're managing a side hustle?
- How can you ensure you are not interrupted?
- Can you share childcare with friends and family so you have free, uninterrupted time?
- Can you switch off from noise or do you need noise?

When you have identified your space, it is also important to set boundaries to protect that space and time. These may be boundaries that you set yourself as well as setting boundaries for those around you. This involves others understanding your goals and knowing how they can support you best – which may simply mean ensuring uninterrupted peace for those sacred hours!

Be sure not to overlook your needs during your thinking and planning time. If you're someone who cannot afford to go over your allotted time – set an alarm. If you cannot work without drink or snacks, plan these in advance so they don't become a disruption to your time and are readily available. If you are easily distracted, set your phone to airplane mode or leave it in another room. If you cannot concentrate if you hear children crying, can someone else take care of your family demands for these golden hours? Your time is precious and having carefully planned and carved it out you simply cannot afford for it to be wasted.

If you are able to set out large chunks of time but tend to procrastinate and find yourself distracted by household chores, make a list of those chores and then use them as your break time. It's not healthy to sit at a laptop for hours on end so when you feel ready for that quick break use it to prep lunchboxes, unload the dishwasher or iron one item of clothing. That way, everything gets done and you are able to take a break, which your creativity mind will certainly welcome. As we discussed at the start of the book – sometimes these mundane tasks are when the unconscious mind takes over and ideas evolve, so when you become stuck those chores may end up being the solution.

I call this planned procrastination – putting all those procrastination chores that are on your mind into a mental list. You can then utilize them productively rather than them becoming a deterrent. This way you also have confidence that things can get done as you go along. Make sure they are only short tasks though – stopping to mow the lawn will really eat into your time a little too much!

By having a healthy approach to balancing your workload, chores and also engaging your support network or setting boundaries with yourself and those around you, this will create a strong structure of control. There will always be times when things go totally out of the window; however, when you know you have a plan to return to the next day or the next week, this should reduce some of the anxiety and pressure at any lost time.

There will no doubt be times when things are out of your control and this is when you have to reflect back on your intention and purpose. Remember why you started. Remember that reflection is not inaction. These short-term 'sacrifices' are not, in fact, sacrifices. They are short-term commitments that carry long-term gains. You have made commitments to focus your time where it adds value. You have carefully planned where you spend your time and have pivoted to a new way of thinking and doing as you forge forwards into a new way of being.

You are becoming an entrepreneur and business owner. When your inner voice suggests that you're missing out on those drinks with friends or you should be spending this time with the family, remember that your commitments now are going to benefit you and your family in the long term. You have created a schedule that allows this balance and accepts these changes. Friends will often fall off along the way if they feel that your priorities have shifted. However, you will be moving towards a future circle of friends with shared goals and passions who will add greater value and inspire you on your journey.

Remember the analogy of the mountain climb. There will always be friends who cheer at the beginning and maybe want to join, but when it gets cold and tough they soon fall off and decide this isn't for them. Their journey isn't your journey and that is fine. What's important is that you stay firmly focused on your journey, knowing that you will soon bump into more climbers who are focused on the same goals and will encourage you when it's tough rather than turn back and head home.

The when?

Launching: is timing everything?

> 'There is no right time, there is just time,
> and what you choose to do with it.' – Unknown

Things are now starting to get real. Let this feeling excite you not terrify you. After all, you've worked so hard to get this far you should enjoy the journey. If you remember your positive affirmations from earlier in the book, then maybe you will have some statements to reflect on in these big moments. You have spent a lot of time planning this moment! You're clear on what you want to do; why you want to do it; where you will do it and how. Now is the biggest question – when will you do it?

This may be the easiest question to answer for the gung-ho entrepreneur and activists amongst you – you'll just do it. We all have those friends who are the first to jump off the cliffs into the sea without so much as a glance at what lies beneath. There are those who take several glances and step back, hesitate and consider the numerous scenario outcomes. There are those who never leap at all. You certainly haven't come this far to not leap at all!

What is the worst that can happen? Even so-called failure at starting a business is not failing if you have learned a million more lessons than those who never take the leap. Starting and not succeeding brings with it far more growth than never starting at all.

One thing's for sure, there's no such thing as perfect timing. If you wait for what seems like the perfect time, you will never start and those days of waiting become weeks, months or maybe years and that's when dreams and ideas die. The conditions will rarely ever be perfect.

We have spent time balancing action and reflection throughout the journey so far. You have spent time shifting between the mountain view and trail view of your journey. There is one other element to this mental preparation and reflection, and this is visualization. Begin to prepare yourself for the moment when you take the leap. It is fast approaching and you need to be ready to jump without hesitation. How can you visualize a perfect launch when the conditions are rarely perfect you may ask?

It's important to remember what elements of starting a business are within your control and those that rely solely on external factors and circumstance. Knowing that you have managed everything within your control, you have to trust and leave the rest to fate to a degree. If you have taken time to focus on mindfulness and built meditation into your practice, I hope that you will have started to build a practice of letting go of those things that are out of your control more easily.

We know that no matter how much you plan something to perfection there will always be curve balls and unexpected situations. The key is not to react to these things but to consider how you will respond to these shifts. If you have ever tried to plan a large event or special occasion, I'm sure this is relatable. What will make the difference to your experience is how you respond. You can waste time and energy getting angry, upset and frustrated when things go wrong or you can realize these things are out of control and think about how it can be avoided in future and how you can leverage what you do have to your advantage as far as possible. Or, when life throws you lemons…

Let us return to the question of timing – the when? There may be other external factors driving the timing of your business launch. You may need to be up and running as you are dependent on an income. You may need to be in business as you see an opportunity with a shift in the environment. Your business may be supported by seasonality, so your window to launch may be time or weather bound. Maybe your business is a seasonal business in itself and it will only operate at certain times of the year. It may also be the case that you feel others will be in the process of starting similar businesses and you want to get into market first. Proceed cautiously with this as very often it's not those who go first that succeed – Google wasn't the first search engine; Facebook wasn't the first social media site. As we discussed previously, be mindful of being driven by competition. Focus solely on your goals and purpose. When you focus on the competition you may find you're distracted from your main priority – the client.

When there are external pressures impacting your start-up, it is easy to get distracted by the environment. Whilst it is important to scan the horizon for shifts in consumer and market trends, it is important to remember that a completed product is better than a perfect one. In your search for perfection you may be missing vital opportunities to engage with your customer or to raise awareness of your brand in the market place. In fact, by the time you are ready to launch you will most likely be thinking of new and better versions of your business prototype already.

If you remember the work you did on brand earlier in the book, you will recall that people buy into ideas. Your product will, and should, evolve. Your brand look and feel may change. Provided that you have done your work on your consumer research, you can take your customers with you on this journey. Once you have built customer loyalty and a solid consumer base, they will happily come along on the journey of change, growth and diversification.

Your customer buys into you first and foremost, quickly followed by your product, your brand and your values. If you have done the hard work on building up the right connections and audience with your potential clients, they will be ready, waiting and expecting something new and evolutionary over time. Take the example of Apple. Its clients now expect change and transformation as this has become the culture and model it has embedded.

It is worth taking some time here to consider how technology can enable your business and equally how it may pose a threat to your business model if you are not continually scanning the horizon for changing trends. As you create various habits around your business that allow you time to also stop and reflect, ensure you take this opportunity to look further afield than your industry alone.

Technology advancements are wide reaching and you may be able to join the dots on how tech capability and development in one field could impact your own industry. Take, for example, the concept of 3D printing. How could that impact your business? The technology being used in blockchain – will this change the way your customers use your product or service or pay for goods and services. Consider the advances in wearable technology. Do you see this having an impact on your business? Is it complementary to your business model or a threat to which you need to adapt?

Technology is not the only possible threat or enabler on the horizon. Being able to identify shifts in consumer sentiment is also important. Movements may start small and build slowly over time; however, they often build up into an almost overnight shift in consumer consciousness. Dismissing these sentiments as fads can be dangerous. Always approach them with a curious mind and consider if you can build these into your business model not only to test your consumer intrigue but also to ensure readiness for a shift.

Scanning the horizon ensures you are not solely internally focused and are able to anticipate change. What appears to be a distant possibility such as cameras being replaced by mobile phones can quickly appear as a risk or sudden shift that impacts your business. As a start-up or new business, the key to success is not only adaptability and change but also anticipating consumers' future needs before they even know they have a need and joining invisible dots. Being curious and exploring solutions to problems that your consumers are not even aware of yet requires adaptability and will often bring a competitive edge.

This does not mean to say that when scanning the horizon and timing your business launch, you should stop or delay. Trends can equally pass and dissolve quickly if we consider how the future of music at one stage shifted from CD to mini disc only to be totally disrupted by the concept of online streaming. The mini disc was not disruptive; it was an alternative but did not solve any consumer need. The key is to keep one eye on the horizon and not underestimate how quickly sentiments or technology can change your business.

When you have taken the time to plan your business journey and built in habits around scanning the horizon, it's time to launch. The consumers are ready and waiting for your product. After all, it's likely you've been talking about it across various forums for some time now. In short – the time is now. There really is no time like the present. Bite the bullet and enjoy the ride, remembering at all times that this was once just an idea in your mind and now it has manifested – that alone is a huge achievement. It's important to look how far you have come! Who knows how far you will go?

**'It's not just about creativity, it's about the person
you're becoming while you're creating.'
– Charlie Peacock**

4

Support systems

Who will help me?

Family, friends and familiarity

> 'Anything is possible when you have the right
> people there to support you.' – Misty Copeland

Being an entrepreneur can seem like a rather lonely journey when you start out, particularly if your idea is visionary and beyond the limits of most people's imagination. When you have your idea and feel fuelled by excitement, it can be difficult to share that passion for all the reasons we covered in Chapter 1, such as doubt, fear and lack of confidence. How can you possibly be an entrepreneur? Now that you have shifted from that mindset and have your positive affirmations in place, it's time to consider who else may form part of your support network.

I use support in this chapter in the widest possible sense. There will be people who you turn to for emotional support right through to technical or production support in bringing your idea to fruition. There is often a tendency to think of support as somewhere you turn when times are tough; however, support is needed in various forms at various times and includes finding your cheerleaders! We will cover each one in some detail and by the end of this chapter you will realize that, in fact, this journey is certainly not one you need or will undertake alone.

The easiest place to start is the support network closest to you in the form of friends and family. This network may need to be reviewed in some detail. Family will usually be understandably biased and supportive of whatever you decide to do. They are not likely to be objective or push you further than you feel you can go. They will tend to be the sympathetic ear that you turn to when you need some words of encouragement, some home-cooked food or a reality check when times get tough. You may also have some family members who are less sympathetic and out of touch with this level of support and may steer you away from your passions and ambitions – steer clear of those who you know will not lend a sympathetic ear when you need it and may end up encouraging you to quit altogether.

Becoming an entrepreneur will certainly shake up your social circle, connections and even friends circle. This is not something to mourn; it is something to embrace. Letting go of the old and moving towards the new is a continuous cycle in life. Whilst friends and family are often more constant, there will be times when even those long-standing constants will shift. It is important to remember that you're on a journey towards something bigger and better and you are growing and changing as a person. There will be friends who don't understand the journey, others who may want to come on the journey but struggle to keep up with you and others will naturally fall away. This prospect may seem a little daunting right now particularly if you value a very tight friendship network. Be prepared for that shift and be comfortable with moving into new circles.

The support that you will need from family and friends will be quite different from that you require professionally in building your business or networking in new circles. The former is safe, it is known, and it is somewhere you can return to and will always be accepted. This is a positive support and crutch that will help you mentally and emotionally. There is then the professional support, which will be a lot more pragmatic and transactional and may over time lead to new and different partnerships and sometimes friendships.

It is worth creating a stakeholder map of your support group to identify where you can go for the different support you need amongst family and friends. There will be those who always see the upside and encourage you no matter what. There will be those who will tell it as it is and not handle you with kid gloves – these are important people too. You need trusted friends or family who will be objective but direct and tell you when they don't like an idea and, more importantly, why – with rationale and logic. Consider if any of your friends or family are your target customer – they may be reflecting back valuable feedback of what your target customer may be thinking. There will also be those who are unable to provide any helpful feedback as their own personal lens distorts their view and they don't really understand your journey – these are friends who want you to stay in your comfort zone and be content with life as it is. You may want to spend less time here and certainly not talk business with them when you do. All of these relationships play an important role and provide different perspectives. Mapping out from the start who you will seek advice from and who you should avoid talking business with altogether can help steer you in the right direction when times get tough. When you're struggling half way up the mountain, you wouldn't turn to someone for advice who thinks you should never have started – you can be pretty certain you should only turn here when you need a reinforcement to quit!

Reflection 12: Support roles

- Consider your current network and contacts.
- Make a list of all your *relevant* contacts including family and friends.

- Categorize the type of support they can offer, e.g. emotional, financial, intellectual, experiential.
- Note down the benefits of using them for support.
- Also note down the limitations of their support, e.g. are they objective? Do they have biases about your product? Do they have biases about your consumer?
- Now list out if there are certain stages of your business where they could support more, e.g. start-up, BAU, crisis, etc.
- Once you have finished this exercise you should be able to identify if there are any gaps in your support network.
- This will also help to steer you towards identifying those support gaps and building them in your network.

Find your tribe

> 'Surround yourself with only people who are going to lift you higher.' – Oprah Winfrey

If you feel that you are not currently surrounded by friends or family who easily share your vision then it's time to step out of that emotional comfort blanket and broaden your circle. Finding your tribe is an important part of becoming an entrepreneur and breaking outside of your comfort zone towards growth results in finding like-minded people on the same journey. We touched on this earlier in the book where we considered how friends may initially like the idea of the mountain climb; however, after the initial excitement falls away, the training starts and things get serious, their interest fades. You could easily quit at this stage and follow the crowd. However, if you are passionate about your journey, you can be confident that you will meet other climbers along the way whose energy will spur you on all the more. Those new journey partners will have taken similar paths, experienced similar challenges and triumphs and made similar commitments to bring them to this point.

So, how do you find your tribe before you're half way up the mountain? The joy of the internet means you are only clicks away from finding your tribe from the comfort of your own home. You don't even need to physically leave the house – many groups function solely in a virtual space. Take some time to review and research business groups, online social groups and forums for entrepreneurs. Many businesses, both local and multinational, particularly financial institutions, often hold free events for entrepreneurs – usually with a view to educating them on financing and funding. Many financial institutions even run start-up programs in communities where you can network and access many different streams of information. This may not be your initial need but you may just find that you meet like-minded people at the event who may form part of your future tribe.

It's important to be focused and selective in where you spend your time. You have spent a lot of time carving out golden hours for your business venture, which can easily be lost searching online with little outcome or benefit – beware the social media rabbit hole! You may want to think about aligning the expansion of your tribe with companies or forums that share similar values to your business. After all, if your business is focused on sustainability and the local forums are focused on mass producing cheap products, it's likely your values won't align. This would not be the tribe for you.

Take some time to review what forums or meetings are happening in your local area, particularly if your business model or values are more locally based and focus on local sourcing, for example. The beauty of Google is that all this research is at the touch of a button – imagine how difficult it was starting a business pre-internet!

It is worth spending some time deciding how many hours each week or month you can allocate to networking and building your connections. Remember that this is an investment in your time, which, if done well, will lay the foundations for a fruitful network that you can leverage throughout the remainder of your business journey. You may even find that some of the new contacts you meet are potential future customers, which can be of great value in bouncing ideas and testing your product on.

As an entrepreneur, your business needs may be hugely different to the next person. As we explored in the first chapter, your idea may be tech focused or sustainability led. You may be offering a product for a very niche consumer. Your idea may be globally marketable but you need time and resources to build your business slowly. Even though the outcomes for these businesses may be very different, there is much commonality in the journey to success.

All businesses, regardless of size, will tend to run through similar start-up cycles. Entrepreneurs need to research the market, identify consumer trends and future needs, and know how to brand and market a product. There may be a focus on patenting your design or expanding your business online. You will need to consider websites and online payments. Maybe you need to certify your product in some way. The entire journey is one of discovery and learning. You may already be something of an expert in your field or have some knowledge of the market environment you are venturing into. It may be totally unknown – many entrepreneurs have ideas for which they have no skills to bring to fruition, but they simply have the conviction that the idea is viable and they will make it happen. Again – much easier in a highly connected virtual world.

The power of proximity

'Proximity is power. If you can get proximity with
people that are the best... the insights they have and
the life experiences they have. They can save you a
decade of time with one insight.' – Tony Robbins

Once you have researched the communities, forums or
online spaces that are aligned to you, your business and
your values, it's important to structure how much time you
will invest in these forums. Once you have allocated time to
invest in this task, start to think about what you want to get
from each intervention or interaction. There is no value in
attending a network event if you want to learn about certain
topics and they aren't discussed. Have some clear questions
ready for the challenges you may be facing or the information
you need. If people in the group can't answer, they are likely
to know someone who can and will signpost you to others in
the same tribe.

The great thing about these forums is that people are
attending them because they either need support or want
to offer their advice and guidance. Be mindful to also sense
check the advice you are receiving. Ask a few people for their
views on the same topic and seek some kind of affirmation
of a solution and then take time to review and research
this further online or with other trusted support members.
One word of advice: if you feel relaxed and comfortable in
a forum and the conversations don't challenge you – leave
this forum. Growth does not happen in your comfort zone.
It's like joining the mountain climbers who are going to
picnic every few hours and enjoy the view, whereas you're
wanting to push on with your climb. If you find a group
who feel outside of your comfort zone, this is where you
need to be. Maybe they are more articulate, commercially
aware and knowledgeable than you. If so, this is where you
need to be. If you're climbing a mountain and find yourself
amongst pros, you will definitely pick up some tips that will

take you out of the beginner category. The same is true of networking. Feel the discomfort and do it anyway – it's the only way you will stretch and grow. You will soon come to realize that you can gain their knowledge simply through the power of proximity.

You may want to consider identifying a mentor for your business journey. Maybe there is already someone you know and admire running a similar business to you who you could approach and formalize a partnership with. Most mentors are willing to share their experiences and views, and simply benefit from the satisfaction of helping others on their journey. Be careful in your selection, a direct competitor would not be a wise choice but maybe someone else who has set up a business and understands the journey of entrepreneurship and the challenges along the way. This person becomes a sounding board, someone who you can share your journey with and ask – what did you do? How would you approach this problem? Is there something I haven't thought of?

You may select different mentors for different stages of your business life cycle as it evolves from start-up to scaling into a large business that may require funding and investment. You will find that as you expand your tribe, you become connected to people with a very diverse skillset and varying levels of expertise. The key is to leverage these as much as possible and be prepared in return to help them when they send someone else your way. Remember that one day you may be the person that someone wants to be mentored by so it's important to give back.

One important thing to consider as you build your network is that whilst some relationships may be more transactional than others, you never know who that person may be connected to. As an entrepreneur, this is an important mindset shift – everyone is a potential customer or certainly knows someone who could be. If you take this mindset into each networking event or forum, you will have a more genuine interest to build deeper connections. You should always remember to ask – do you know anyone who would be interested in this product? Who knows where that simple question may lead? Connections are so valuable and can open doors to the very people who can help fast track your business success. Imagine if you attended an event and the one person you didn't speak to was looking to invest in your kind of product!

This comes to another important point – your pitch. The reflections you have completed to date can help you in perfecting your pitch. The clarity you have established around your intention, purpose, brand and values can all be leveraged in pitching your business and networking. This is the time to utilize the outputs and content from the exercise to describe your business in an inspiring and passionate way for those who don't know you or your product. We will explore the concept of pitching and what makes a perfect pitch in Chapter 6.

Remember that every interaction is an opportunity to convey your brand, your values and those of the business. If you talk about the sustainability of the environment being critical to your values but sit with a plastic water bottle in front of you, this will not resonate with your audience. The values and branding that you created have to be lived and breathed, any incongruence will soon become evident when you start to go out into the world and publicize them. It would be like having an overweight and out-of-shape personal trainer. They may be perfectly knowledgeable on how to lead a healthy lifestyle and train; however, it would be difficult to buy into a vision of health and fitness from them if they are not exuding something you can aspire to.

Feedback

**'We all need people who will give us feedback.
That's how we improve.' – Bill Gates**

I'm sure you will have heard the phrase 'feedback is a gift'. It certainly is, but how it is wrapped, how you process it and what you do with it needs careful consideration. The good news is you control what feedback you take on board and what you do with it. This also comes with a degree of caution – some feedback you may not want to hear; however, if the source is trusted and the intention is right, it may be exactly the feedback you need to hear. Whilst it may be difficult to swallow, listening to feedback that is challenging and uncomfortable may just lead you to make the right decisions for your business at critical points in time. Again, it's important to remember the stakeholder support reflection earlier in this chapter. You have to know the source of the feedback and whether that feedback is objective or biased, especially when it's in your favour. It would be akin to climbing a mountain and having your friends feed back that you're doing a good job, whereas an objective professional climber may say you're getting something wrong and need to change course. The most valuable feedback to progress would, in fact, be the latter.

Knowing which feedback to take on board, what needs to be heard and what will help you and your business grow is something that takes practice. This is where your reflections earlier in the chapter will help you to process what is objective and helpful or biased and skewed. The brain receives thousands of pieces of information to process every second, and it takes a rather lazy approach by sorting out that which is familiar and known and relying on past experience to provide a similar reaction when experienced repeatedly. When you are receiving feedback, depending on the source, it may not be as clear or direct as you need it to be. You may need to question and explore it further.

Feedback is a critical part of your business journey as well as your personal growth as an entrepreneur. You will get feedback from family, friends, mentors, network events, customers and no doubt competitors and objectors to your cause. All are relevant pieces of feedback and some are more relevant than others. You will also find you get conflicting feedback so it's important to consider how you will deal with this. Will you dismiss the negative or constructive feedback and digest the positive only or will you give consideration to the constructive views in case there is an opportunity to improve your product as a result?

Feedback is such a broad-ranging topic that you cannot establish a definitive response plan. What you can do, however, is prepare yourself with a few questions so that each time you get feedback you have a means of triaging it by relevance or importance. Consider the below:

- Is this feedback from someone who I trust / has expertise on this subject?
- Is this feedback I have heard before from the same or different stakeholder group?
- How can I better understand what is driving this feedback?
- Could this feedback be shared by more customers who are simply not speaking up?
- Could an interaction with this person add value to my growth or understanding?

There may be other questions you would like to add to this list. I would suggest you have just four or five questions that you can remember so that when you receive feedback you can quickly triage. You may decide to have a few triage groups – dismiss the feedback altogether, explore the feedback in more detail or accept the feedback and act on it. The way you triage is determined by you – just ensure it is an objective training process. Robust questions should help this process where you feel an emotional response as a first reaction.

Whilst most feedback you will receive will be clear and direct, it's also important to pay attention to more subliminal feedback. When you consider your online platforms, are certain products receiving less traffic, views or likes? This does not always mean that there's an issue but you may want to sense check with some targeted communications with customers or trusted stakeholders for clearer feedback. Being aware of the subtleties of feedback is important. People may be too polite to say they don't like the taste, look or colour of your product. It may convey an image they don't like. Be prepared to probe more when feedback appears as a quiet voice or silence.

Reflection 13: Feedback map

- Who are your current stakeholders?
- This may be a much broader or different list than those in your support network and may be more consumer and business based.
- Categorize your stakeholders into types such as advocates, competitors, primary or secondary consumers – be mindful of your own biases in categorizing them.
- Consider what types of feedback each stakeholder can provide – product based, personal, environmental or market-based.
- Consider and document how much you would consider, respect or disregard their feedback and challenge yourself as to why.
- Are your own biases stopping you from hearing valuable feedback?
- How could these different perspectives add value to you and your business?
- When faced with challenges, refer to this map to consider where you may gauge the most appropriate feedback.

One topic we haven't covered is what to do if the network or forum you need doesn't seem to exist. Is there something missing that would help you and your business, as well as others on a similar journey or with similar interests? This in itself is a potential opportunity. Whatever your business, if there are no existing relevant forums, why not create one? There may be many like-minded individuals in want of such a group but simply haven't the time to put something in place. Equally, don't get sidetracked. Something simple such as an online forum or introductory group meeting in person in a local venue may open up your network sufficiently for you to progress and expand your network. And if no one shows up – simply use the time for working on your business. Something very informal in a coffee shop is a great way to sense interest and could just lead to a single but valuable connection. The entrepreneurial journey is one of continual trial and error – one shot in the dark at establishing a group could be a huge benefit and open up a potential customer base. It may also not take off and nothing has been lost in time or energy. Having a nothing to lose and everything to gain mindset really helps with these small leaps in the dark.

Expertise: build, borrow or buy?

> 'Don't be intimated by what you don't know. That can be your greatest strength and ensure that you do things differently from everyone else.'
> – Sarah Blakely

Before you set out on this journey, there would no doubt have been a million reasons you told yourself as to why you couldn't be an entrepreneur. You have a great idea but there are so many things you don't know about starting, running and owning a business. So far, those doubts on what, why, when, where and how have already been tackled in the first few chapters. As you start to explore this support phase, you should begin to realize that it isn't a solo journey. The question of 'who?' will help you is not only limited to the emotional support network established in the previous pages. There is also a plethora of technical support that needs consideration.

Again, imagine starting a business pre-internet and reflect on how many questions can now be answered at the press of a button. You no longer need to spend hours researching content; there is so much you can learn and research online for free. You can take time to teach yourself how to build a website and buy a domain name, etc. You don't need to be able to code! There are so many things that have become accessible and many are still free.

Also sense check your emotional support groups – they may contain the expertise you need or be connected to others with the technical skills you may need at various stages of your start-up. This may be where your mentor relationship comes in, providing guidance of their experience and signposting you to solutions. All these resources are accessible and free.

You may even have made those social connections through online forums and expanded your support network out to those who have the knowledge and expertise you are lacking.

Simply engaging with them and asking questions may be all you need to point you in the right direction. If we refer to our mountain climb analogy, it's no different to having made transactional relationships with other climbers, and as you pass them later on your climb you simply ask which route is better or how their hike has been. Most people on the same journey would be happy to share any tips and pitfalls to help you avoid them.

You should be starting to see how the investment in network and forums / communities will have a huge benefit, and no doubt you will soon find yourself also sharing your knowledge and experience with others setting off on similar journeys. You will already be the more experienced climber to the person just setting out – already you have things to share and ways to help. In time, you may even become a mentor. No one's journey should be in isolation; by supporting others we achieve so much more and you will also find that it helps to build your own confidence.

So, what happens when you have finally exhausted your networks and are unable to perform some of the more complicated tasks that are simply not your forte? Maybe you don't have the time to spend hours learning new skills. Your start-up schedule is already limited and spending time on learning new skills may prolong the launch of your business and this may not be an option for you.

There comes a time when you need to weigh up build versus buy. If someone else has the skill and capability to deliver what you need in one hour why spend 20 hours researching and trying to learn yourself? This is where you need to consider whether it is of more value to buy the skill than learn the skill yourself. By investing an hour in a robust discussion with a website designer, you could save yourself endless hours of time, money and frustration all of which are a distraction to your creative energy.

It is worth briefly mentioning budgeting at this stage. So far, the tools and resources to plan and prepare your business start-up to date have been free and leveraged through networks. There will, however, come a point where you need to spend some money on investing in your set up or launch. Even if you plan to seek investment in your business start-up, it is likely that it will not have come to fruition at this stage in the journey. You may have potential investor interest if you have been networking well and building significant focus around your brand. For the purpose of this process and business planning, we will assume this isn't the case and that funding has not been secured. If you do have a loan or investor interest you will still need to manage budgets.

When budgeting, always build a buffer – costs often spiral out of control so consider a 10% buffer on top and if you never need to use it consider that a bonus. The last thing you want is for things to stop when you have momentum because you didn't budget correctly or plan for certain delays or challenges. We will explore budgeting in more detail in Chapter 5.

If you simply don't have the money to buy skills then learning is not the only option. You may be able to exchange expertise and skills with someone else. Think about the skills you have that someone else would need or possibly pay for and leverage these. It may be as simple as offering to read documents and give feedback. If your business is fitness based, offer some free coaching in exchange for a website build. There are even websites that facilitate such exchanges – you can actively advertise what you have to offer and what skills you need. It's a great way to exchange your time for mutual benefit with others.

Swapping skills does not have to be through a formalized website exchange program. You may be able to leverage your support networks to exchange skills. If your business is tech focused but you're not strong in writing content, maybe you have someone in your network who can write some content for your branding in exchange for some website advice. There are so many ways to overcome the need to buy skills. Just try them out – you'd be surprised how willing people are to reciprocate or even just help for the good karma! Remember – they may be a future customer for you and you may be a future potential customer for them one day. With this mindset, every interaction and offer of support exchanged could be sowing seeds for something much bigger and better in the future.

Reflection 14: Bargaining and budgeting – time and money

Break down the skill you need to buy and understand the average hourly costs for these skills.

- How many hours will you need?
- Is there a cheaper alternative or is quality key?
- What skills can you offer up for exchange?
- What will be my space costs or have I found free alternatives?
- Do I need premises to evolve my business or operate my business?
- How much would I need in order to pay for this for the first 12 months?
- Are utilities included?
- Are the premises insured or would I need to cover or contribute to insurances of any kind?
- What skills do I need that I have the time and capacity to learn?
- What skills do I need to buy?
- Where can I get these skills and know they are verified?
- Can I find recommendations from my networks?
- Can I exchange skills within my networks?

If you are prepared to set time aside or have no option other than to learn the skills, don't see this as a barrier on your journey, see this as an opportunity. You will learn so much in the process you may even end up managing your business differently because you have had to go through the learning journey yourself rather than taking shortcuts. You may just create a new perspective by taking this route and the skills that you have to offer in future as an exchange become much broader. If you do go on to mentor others on this journey you will add far more value having taken the long route.

5

Know your business

How will I grow my expertise?

Empowerment for growth

'Always walk through life as if you have something new to
learn, and you will.' – Vernon Howard

When you invest in buying expertise and in the skills of
others, rather than learning them, it often creates an element
of dependency on others, which becomes costly when things
go wrong.

When you take the time to learn a new skill from start to
finish, you will be more adept at troubleshooting if something
doesn't go to plan and, more often than not, you can solve
the issue without the need for expertise or intervention. If
you are the first climber to scale a mountain, you will learn
and grow much more than those who follow and take the
path well known. Going first is always the hardest, but can be
the most rewarding.

The balance between buying expertise and building your
own knowledge is a question of personal preference and
is often largely driven by time and cost. For time-poor and
cash-rich entrepreneurs, the best solution may be to buy in
expertise; however, for those entrepreneurs who are cash

and time poor, you may need to prepare to climb the steep north face alone.

Don't be deterred by this challenge. It could be the best route for you and your business in the long term. Some of the most successful entrepreneurs have taken this route and often share how this more challenging journey helped them and their business to grow and adapt more effectively. Sarah Blakely, the founder of Spanx, frequently talks of her journey and how teaching herself skills that other entrepreneurs may have bought prepared her to better respond to customer feedback for improvements to her product later down the line. Had she not scaled the north face, she would not have been equipped with the knowledge to overcome future problems and provide the solutions.

If you have identified that you need to buy expertise, be sure not to write this off as fully outsourced and closed. The outsourcing may allow you to progress with other matters but be sure to revisit them in time and get to understand the skill. The more you empower yourself to understand all elements of your business, the better prepared you will be when challenges arise. No one else should know your business better than you, this is your idea and your dream so be sure to hold onto that.

Choosing the right partnerships and developing relationships with your outsourced support can be a key driver of your success and future development as a business owner. In the same way that you may hire a mountain guide to plan your route, ultimately, there will come a time when your knowledge level and expertise develops to the point where they are no longer needed. The guide knows this, yet does not decline your business knowing that their guidance will ultimately make them redundant. Their business model will be based on knowing you operate in similar circles of interest where their expertise and your experience with them will result in recommendations and further business.

Outsourcing should not equate to disinterest. Whilst you may rely on the expertise of others to ensure you get things right, be sure to take an interest and learn from their expertise. When you first climb a mountain, you will no doubt rely on the guide to navigate and you may blindly follow, content that you are in safe hands. The more you climb, however, the more curious you should become. Notice how they read maps, and ask questions when they choose certain routes or paths or equipment for challenging parts of the climb. Question why, and get to understand their thinking and approach.

Curiosity leads to understanding and growth. In the same way that you may want to outsource your accounts because you have not quite solidified your affirmation that you can do maths! This doesn't mean you shouldn't spend time with your accountant to develop a partnership whereby they can help you to learn, grow and develop.

Often, as a novice sets out to climb a mountain, they overpack with too many clothes, too many items, too many comfort gadgets that they just won't utilize and all the baggage simply adds weight to the climb. So, you gratefully bestow these excesses upon a Sherpa and outsource thinking to your guide. Over time, the more you climb the more efficiently you plan and prepare and your need for a Sherpa comes only when you are truly struggling and need to lighten the load.

You will also find that if you are not climbing the mountain alone, between you and other climbers, you have the combined skills needed. You may become the navigation expert and have a co-climber who is great with ropes. Be sure to continually develop your expertise as this will empower you to become self-sufficient as a fully rounded business owner.

As an entrepreneur, your business will, however, progress through cycles. Each stage of your business is like setting off on a new mountain climb and you may need to be fully equipped with Sherpa and guide. Over time, the need for the guide and Sherpa will subside. You come to realize the Sherpa was a comfort blanket bringing everything you thought you needed just in case you hit a bump in the journey.

As you progress through these cycles, your knowledge and confidence will grow. Your dependency will decrease and you become Sherpa, guide and climber in one. Even if the next summit has new challenges, you will be more likely to try the route alone only calling in expertise of the guide for small parts of the journey.

The more you get to know your business and face these challenging aspects, the more informed your decisions around business growth and change will become. You will be better equipped to manage future challenges or setbacks as well as planning for growth and expansion. The growth that you find outside of your comfort zone will broaden your skillset as a business owner. The broader your skillset the easier each mountain climb becomes.

Budgeting for beginners

**'A budget is telling your money where to go
instead of wondering where it went.' – Dave Ramsay**

Many entrepreneurs are by nature creative and visionary. They have big ideas that can change the world, small ideas that can change the life within a community or product ideas that can add value to healthcare or save the environment. Many entrepreneurs already have ideas about secondary phases of their business before their initial product is even launched. They are often high energy, charismatic and passionate about their product and their ability to change the world for the better no matter how large or small their idea.

Such energetic and creative minds are, more often than not, less inspired by the idea of a sitting down with a spreadsheet! Yet, budgeting and planning are equally, if not more critical, to business success than ideation. Many entrepreneurs who overlook this essential phase, often launch products or ideas into the market that cannot be sustained. The price point may be too high for the target consumer or the materials and distribution are too expensive to meet the selling price. It may be that the product is such a success that supply cannot meet demand and customers are left disappointed. Without planning, your business idea can quickly emerge in the market through a competitor product that can be mass produced, shipped globally and all at lower cost. This is also a great reason to ensure products are patented!

Avoiding the scale-up issues or managing supply and demand may be partially solved with investment support. As your business grows, you may consider selling your product or service to larger organizations, partnering with distributors or utilizing established supply chains. To enter into such partnerships, you will need to fully understand your financials and the feasibility of these partnerships. We will explore this a little later when we look at the idea of pitching. In the meantime, budgeting is critical to get your product or idea to the point of sale without placing you or your business in financial risk.

For entrepreneurs, many will see the journey as an overnight success and aspire to a notion that entrepreneurship is a get-rich-quick approach to business. Everyone gets to see the triumphant summit picture, yet few will appreciate the long climb and the planning, trials and tribulations along the journey to get to that successful summit point. The planning behind the mountain climb is critical to the success of the climb itself. Reflection is not inaction and preparation is not the antithesis of progress. This approach applied to your time spent budgeting and planning could be the key to the successful launch or expansion of your business.

Budgeting basics

> 'Don't tell me what you value, show me your budget,
> and I'll tell you what you value.' – Joe Biden

So, what is a budget and how do you start to plan your budget?
A budget is simply a plan for the future – and this book is all
about planning and preparation! The only difference here is
that you are dealing with numbers not ideas. If you're not a
fan of numbers or have come to tell yourself you aren't good
with maths, then keep pushing through this chapter and you
will certainly come out the other side feeling more confident.
Remember your positive affirmations? You probably can
do numbers but maybe you need more time or need some
support to check you're on the right track. So do the work
and then use your support networks to help check your
understanding and workings.

Let's take a look at the various elements of a budget. Where
many people get deterred is when financial terminology
comes into play so we will break down the financial language
into simple terms. There are four key elements to a budget:
sales revenue, fixed costs, variable costs and profit.

Sales revenue is simply your estimated sales or projected sales
in the planning phase or actual sales once your business is
launched.

Fixed costs are those costs that are typically just that! Costs
that largely stay the same regardless of the amount of sales
you generate, such as employee salaries, rents and utilities.

Variable costs may change throughout the year such as the
price of packaging, shipping, supplies. If you are providing
a service, the cost of providing that service may change (e.g.
accommodation and travel costs may increase).

Profit is simply the sales amount minus fixed costs and minus
variable costs.

If you are able to understand these key principles then you can create a budget!

With these four elements in mind, let's think about your business, broadly from start to finish, and try to understand the potential costs at each stage in order to help you build a budget and understand the costs of establishing your business and whether you need significant funding or investment.

You may want to set out to climb Everest, but when you see the costs you realize that maybe it's not feasible. When you then look at your budget you have to build in options – do I scale a smaller mountain and gain the same sense of achievement? Can I compromise on the quality of my equipment to save costs? Can I use less-experienced guides? Can I get sponsorship to lighten the cost burden? If you believe in your idea, you may just need to tailor your immediate goals and start small, whilst keeping your eye on the ultimate goal.

The five stages of business

In order to help you budget effectively longer term, you may want to consider each of the stages of your business and then draft budgets against each stage. If you feel overwhelmed by this long-term planning or that the costs are building up, don't be deterred. When your business moves from the seed stage, there are always ways to source investment and financial support. Your foresight and planning on future budgets will be an integral part of your pitch.

In order to know which mountain you should aim for, it's important to understand each of the stages of your business to be able to plan and budget for each phase. The five key stages of business are 'seed', start-up, growth, established and expansion. We will explore these briefly.

The **seed** stage, as the name suggests, is the stage when your business is no more than an idea. A seed requires many more elements in order to grow into something more. Without any intervention it remains simply as a seed. The purpose of this book is to ensure that does not happen! You are a budding entrepreneur, and it is important that ideas do not die.

Start-up is the stage where products are being made or services are being sold. You will have your first customers, a small market presence and a small cash flow to manage.

In the **growth** stage, revenue and customer numbers are on the rise and often a steep rise. Your finances will largely be supported by banks or partnerships and profits start to feed into your budgeting process.

Once this steep growth period slows down, your business will pass into the **established** stage where business is still thriving but the growth is manageable compared to the surge experienced in the growth stage. Your clients and consumers are loyal and well established and financial resource is sourced primarily through banks, investors and profits.

The next natural phase of business for many entrepreneurs is diversification or **expansion**. This is where new ideas or services emerge and you may even explore new markets or joint ventures with other companies. This new path can see financial relationships extend to new investors and partners.

Most readers will be expected to be at the seed stage and we will therefore spend more time exploring this phase of budgeting. Once you have mastered the principles of budgeting, these can be equally applied to the other stages of business.

Seed stage budgeting

Businesses at this stage tend to rely on self-financing from the entrepreneur and their immediate support circles. Before you secure any loans or ask for financial support, it is important to be clear on your budget plan. Let's take a look at some of the potential costs at this stage of your journey.

Before you have created your product or service, it is likely you will want a website or online forum to sell or communicate about your product or service. Are you able to create a website yourself or will this incur a cost? If you set up your own website, you will still need to pay for the domain name. The name of the website will come at a price. Have you researched what you would like to call your business and whether those domains are available? Some domains with popular words are more expensive than others so be careful when choosing your company name and brand.

Whether your company is local or global, it is likely you will need an online presence to increase awareness of your brand. Whilst social media channels can be utilized in the initial stages, the content is often restricted by word count or is a medium that is simply scrolled through where detail isn't consumed. As your business expands, you may also find you have broader business ideas or interlinked products that may sit well under an umbrella website.

Have you designed your own logo and branding? We explored brand earlier in the book and how important it can be in supporting your product. Do you need expertise to help you design a logo or streamline for your product? What are the costs of design input? Usually your design is a one-off fee. Do you need to only copyright your logo or brand or would you want to consider a trademark to protect the specific features of the brand or logo down to the slightest details?

Let's now consider the development of your product or service. What are the underlying costs associated with creating that product or service? We will consider two examples and then work through a reflection exercise that will allow you to really dive into the costs associated with your product or service development in more detail in order to inform your budgeting process.

Let's take a product example first. If you are creating a new product or piece of technology from scratch, you will no doubt need to bring together a number of component parts. This will involve sourcing the products, shipping the products to a location and assembling them. It may also then involve distributing or delivering that product direct to customers or to your partners for onward distribution. Will you have economies of scale over time? The more products you ship, the more likely the reduction in costs per unit.

Consider a service-based option. It may be that you are providing training services to a customer. Whilst the training relies purely on your presence, there are a number of elements to consider when pricing your service such as travel, accommodation, your own salary, preparation time. Remember your client is paying for your years of experience and credibility not just one hour of delivery time. Be sure to reflect this in your costing. Budgeting is not just important for you to sell a product but also important for you to know how to price your own skills and expertise as a commodity. What is the value of you?

Your service may require you or other contributors to put together material or content for delivery. Their time will need to be costed for content creation. Is this a one-off cost or ongoing cost? Do you or your team members need to travel and deliver the service in person? Can the service be delivered virtually to save costs or increase reach? Is your content protected from duplication with copyright? Do you need legal support to establish contracts with other service providers or partner companies? Do the contracts cover both parties for delivery failures? Do you also have back-up resource in the event of a service not being provided on time?

There are many costs that may be location or industry specific and it is impossible to cover all elements within your business budget. Whilst not all elements can be covered here, be sure to research the local regulations regarding business set up in your country or geography. Do you need a specific licence, visa or permit to operate your business? Are there regulations you must comply with such as health and safety or food safety regulations? Do you require certain qualifications or credentials as the owner of that business? It is likely your business will need to be registered for tax purposes. If you are shipping products in from other geographies have you researched importation costs or taxes on those products? Do you need to ship your product? What alternatives do you have if that company or country is unable to ship your product for any period of time?

When you have taken time to explore all the different costs that will impact your budgets, be sure to leverage your networks and sense check your work within your support groups. Reach out to those people who you have established as mentors. Maybe you have business owners in your network that you can engage with to review your budget lines. Your online forums and networks can also be a great source of information and advice, and if it all feels a little overwhelming take time out with your support system for reassurance and reflect back to your purpose and intention. Remember why you started. The key to budgeting is always to build in a buffer. This ensures that if you overspend or have overlooked a budget line you should be able to quickly compensate for this without any detrimental business impact.

Reflection 15: Budgets, costs and profit

- What is your expected sales revenue for the first 12 months? 24 months? 36 months?
- What are some of your fixed costs?

- List them all even if you don't have the numbers yet for those costs. Start to list all your budget lines. (You may want to start to do this in a spreadsheet alongside your reflection tool – there is an example of a basic budgeting spreadsheet available online.)
- What are your variable costs?
- What is the unit price of your product?
- What are the unit prices for each of your services?
- What would be your profit based on the first 12 months?
- What cost items can be sourced for free or at a cheaper rate?
- Highlight the costs where you need to do more research and explore suppliers.
- Once you have listed all your costs check that you have grouped them correctly into fixed costs and variable costs.
- Start to research actual providers against each budget line to build up an idea of the market price of sourcing your product or charging for your service.
- Don't forget to consider a margin for VAT or tax and also fluctuations in price. Always err on the side of caution rather than underestimate costs.

It is often normal for entrepreneurs to not make a profit in the initial stages of their business. Many businesses even lose money in the first year. However, clearly, this is not a sustainable model and the better you can plan, budget and market your product the greater your chances of success. Having completed the reflection exercise, you can revisit whether you need to increase your sales revenue estimate. It is good to have some different projections of sales numbers required to drive a profit or at least a break-even situation in year one. This will help feed into our later exploration of sales funnel principles.

Business model basics

'Luck is not a business model.'
– Anthony Bourdain

Having understood the key elements of a budget and the various stages of a business, it's important to understand your business model. There are four types of business model often referred to as acronyms B2C, B2B, C2B and C2C. As an entrepreneur, you will need to have an understanding of each as, ultimately, you will be engaged in most of these models throughout your business lifecycle.

Business to consumer (B2C) is the most common business model. A business sells its product or service directly to a consumer, such as a farmer selling in a local market. In a business-to-business (B2B) model, a business will sell its product or service to another business that, more often than not, will then sell this on to the consumer. For example, a local farmer may supply to a supermarket chain, which then sells the product on to the customer.

Consumer-to-business (C2B) is where a consumer creates value and businesses consume that value – we have seen this utilized extensively with the emergence of social media influencers. An example would be where chefs would plug the locally sourced farm product in a recipe and the farmer ultimately benefits from the increase in sales.

Consumer-to-consumer (C2C) businesses have grown exponentially as a result of digital platforms where buyers and sellers are connected directly. This may be a platform where a local farmer sells their product online but may also purchase items online for their product. Effectively, the difference between B2C and C2C is that in the latter example a platform enables a buyer to be a seller and vice versa.

From seed to growth

Having explored budgets, business models and the key stages of the business cycle it's important to understand your key business drivers. Whilst your broader long-term measures of success will be explored in Chapter 7, we will first take time to understand how the various elements of your business connect towards your financial goals. Sales forecasting, pricing and sales funnels which map your customer journey. These key principles will help you to understand how to grow your business.

Sales forecasting is critical in managing your inventory and cash flow to plan for future growth. A clear plan on expected sales will help you to track progress daily, weekly and monthly. This will be a clear indicator, although not the only one, of whether your business is on track or whether you need to focus more on marketing your product or building brand awareness.

When making sales forecasts you may need to make some assumptions and it's important to note these down. When you look back at your sales data you can then also understand the context and environment that was impacting sales at that period. There may be current or future regulatory changes impacting your product sales or service, there could be environmental changes or competitor activity. Be sure to scan the horizon and make a note of the environment both in forecasting and in retrospect.

The basic ingredients of a sales forecast include:

- The period of time over which you expect to sell your product or service.
- An estimated number of sales for that period.
- The revenue for those sales (multiply your unit price by the number of items you expect to sell).
- Your gross sales are the total amount.

- Your net sales are the total amount minus any expenses or cost of production that we explore in the budgeting section previously.

Pricing

Your product or service price may also fluctuate depending on external factors or the life cycle of your business. There are many different types of pricing, which a simple internet engine search will reveal. However, there are three types of pricing that are most relevant for an entrepreneur to consider: demand pricing, competitive pricing and cost-plus pricing.

Demand pricing, as its name suggests, means that your product prices increase based on external factors such as seasonality, weather, disasters or availability. Anyone who tried to purchase sports equipment in the pandemic will certainly have seen evidence of demand pricing at its peak.

Competitive pricing focuses on setting your price based on other similar or competition products. This approach should be used with caution – your product may be of higher value or quality and you need to ensure you don't override any profits by taking this approach.

Cost-plus pricing is probably the best known and utilized of the pricing models. You simply take the cost of producing your goods or service and add a mark up to ensure that you generate a profit with every sale. Provided you have accounted for all production costs in your budgeting, this will always ensure you operate in profit.

A **sales funnel** is the process a consumer goes through from the moment you capture their awareness through to their purchase. There are four key stages – **awareness, interest, decision and action**. The concept of a funnel is that you may get lots of consumers in at the top end but only a percentage will pass through to the final stage and actually purchase. The more interest you can generate at the top end, the higher the chance of converting those to sales at the bottom end.

If you are struggling to meet your sales forecast, it is important to review the sales funnel. Is there more that you can be doing to build product or service awareness? What more can you do to bring customers to your website or market your product or service? Do you have great footfall at your website but this is not converting to sales – do you need to gain more customer feedback on what is deterring their purchasing?

Reflection 16: Generating sales

Consider the below questions:

- Who in your support network is an idea person or a creative? Engage them in this exercise!
- What more can you do to expand the top of your sales funnel?
- Who are your secondary consumers or organizations / businesses that you could target?
- What more can you do to bring customers to your website?
- What has worked well before?
- Are different pricing options now a consideration?
- Can you partner with a local business to drive sales?
- What other marketing opportunities exist for your product or service that you haven't explored?
- Do you have great footfall at your website but this is not converting to sales? Do you need to gain more customer feedback on what is deterring their purchasing?
- Is your latest customer feedback still relevant?

The success of your business is based on a number of metrics coming together in synchronicity. When one part of that chain falters, you need to be ready to adapt. Understanding each of these stages will help you to analyse where your start-up may have challenges for the consumer and enables you to focus on fixing the relevant part based on facts, data and feedback. Being able to adapt your business as you progress from seed to growth is critical and we explored adaptability earlier in the book. Whilst being able to respond to change and feedback is important, you can also plan ahead and anticipate potential challenges. Business continuity planning enables you to operate in a proactive state rather than waiting for feedback or change to arise. Stopping to take a mountain view and scenario planning will enable a smoother climb when issues arise. You can, however, also plan ahead for potential challenges through business continuity planning.

Business continuity planning

**'You don't lose if you get knocked down,
you lose if you stay down.' – Muhammad Ali**

One thing's for certain, business never stands still. You may already find you have new ideas and your product may, in fact, almost be outdated by the time you get to launch. This should not deter you. As you build traction with your first product, you can quickly provide the consumer with enhanced alternatives.

Trends are constantly changing. Your consumer is expecting innovative solutions and modifications to existing products. There are waves of new technology that take over and you need to ensure that you are spending time researching and scanning the horizon not only when in start-up but also during each of the stages of business. This future focused time will ensure you are not caught out by a sudden shift in sentiment from your consumer and will allow you to adapt and respond to changes. Being future focused allows you to plan and prepare and trial potential new ideas on the horizon and see how consumers are responding.

The planning and discipline to get you this far needs to be redirected towards allocating time to monitoring the environment and the future of your market. As your business expands you may find opportunities for more partnerships and collaborations with complementary products, venues or events.

There is often a fear from entrepreneurs of their product taking off too fast for them to be able to meet demand. Turn this fear into excitement – what if your business takes off so much that demand soars? Isn't that the ultimate goal? The pace at which your product takes off may not always be in your control you simply have to be as ready to adapt and shift as possible. Few successful products have a slow steady rise. There often comes a peak point where production has to increase tenfold.

What is your plan for increasing production? Have you considered and researched if your suppliers could manage this shift? How quickly could you get the product to market with a sizeable shift in demand? Does your product require change or assembly that can be outsourced? The answer to these questions is critical to know that you can scale your business quickly in the event of a surge in sales.

If one supplier cannot produce at the rate you need, do you have an alternative supplier who can provide the same quality even if the price point may vary? Does the shift in price point impact your margin significantly? Does your business or product rely on shipping or import of parts? Is it possible to fast track this or are you simply beholden to this timeline in the process? Do you have contingency for ordering locally even if there is a cost impact to at least manage an interim increase in demand?

This is what knowing your business looks like. Being adaptable and able to maintain business continuity with little or no impact to the customer is crucial to maintaining customer loyalty. A production delay or discontinuation of a product can quickly result in consumers simply finding solutions elsewhere. We have all experienced that out-of-stock item in a supermarket that drives us to find alternatives and can switch our entire shopping habits.

Business continuity planning is important for small businesses and start-ups. Whilst the landscape is continually changing and plans can become quickly outdated, it is helpful to have some back-up plans for your sourcing needs. When identifying suppliers or partners that your business relies upon, be sure to retain a list of second options. These can be your backup. Checking in on these partners on a quarterly or biannual basis to sense check prices and capability is a good practice. You may even find they have become more competitive than your preferred choice.

Having considered the above, how quickly could you scale your business? Being able to answer this question and getting clarity on reflection exercise 17 will help you when we look at pitching in Chapter 6.

Reflection 17: Business continuity planning

- Who are you dependent on to deliver your business, service or product?
- Now create a simple table with two columns.
- On one side list all your current business suppliers and dependencies and the other side your continuity and alternative options.
- Do you have alternative supplier contacts for each element?

- Are you clear on the quality and cost of the alternatives?
- What are the key benefits for each supplier (e.g. speed to production, delivery times)?
- Is there any compromise when you use an alternative that may impact your product quality?
- Would you need to alter your selling price as a result to ensure consumer trust?
- Is there a way to outsource assembly locally on a pay-per-item basis rather than fixed cost?
- Try to capture all the possible outcomes and alternatives and knock on impact of the business as usual column being impacted.

If your business is service based or requires in-person interaction, consider how you can be accessible to customers virtually. Can you offer online solutions when your own time becomes maximized? Is there a virtual online option or alternative for your consumers to utilize rather than miss out? Consider having your content online in pay-to-view tutorials – these may be at a reduced price compared to your in-person offering and provide a way to retain customers when they want your service. Having these options ready to roll out will ensure that you don't miss out on onboarding new customers.

Whatever your current business model, consider how you could make it accessible and virtual. It may need to take a slightly different shape, form or cost, but being ready for such surges in demand is important. Equally, a virtual offering can ensure readiness in times when you cannot deliver your service in person such as during a pandemic or disaster.

So you see, your journey as an entrepreneur is really only just beginning. There are so many exciting opportunities ahead to collaborate, expand and diversify your business, product or service. Let this opportunity excite you not terrify you. The extent to which you engage with this new opportunity remains fully in your control. Ignoring these opportunities altogether, however, may result in you losing customers to those who are constantly adapting and innovating. Even if a product is not as superior, if it is more accessible consumers will sometimes compromise. Let's look at how you can maximize every opportunity to sell your ideas in the next chapter.

6

Pitch perfect preparation

How do I sell my idea?

'Sell ideas. Not stuff.'
– Aaron Ross

Having spent time exploring business models, the life cycle of a business and budgeting, you should feel more at ease explaining your own business model and product or service with confidence. When it comes to finally selling your product and talking to potential customers, you will need to be equally clear, confident and concise when answering that all important question, 'What do you do?'.

Every person you meet is a potential customer or may open the door to another business opportunity. Pitching is not limited to investment situations. It extends to every conversation you have as a business owner. Every interaction or connection may lead to a sale or partnership. Being ready to pitch your product or service succinctly and clearly to invite further intrigue is a critical skill.

Whether your business will be self-funded, require investment or will simply grow through word of mouth or online presence, the following chapter will help you to understand the importance of really knowing your customer and the market in which you operate.

When you decide to climb a mountain, you would typically research the location, weather, challenges with transport and the local facilities on offer. Understanding your market is no different when setting up a business. You need to know what is happening in and around your business environment. How is technology impacting your market? Is new GPS technology negating the need for a guide? Can climbers use transport to avoid lower levels of the climb and save their energy for the harder stages? Knowing the context before you climb and knowing your market before you launch your business is critical.

In order to pitch confidently and with sound evidence of your research, you will need to be able to demonstrate clear insights about the market in which you want to operate and the trends, challenges and expectations of your consumer. Let's explore these in some more detail before we return to the pitch process.

Know the market

> 'Progress is impossible without change, and those who cannot change their minds cannot change anything.'
> – George Bernard Shaw

Whether you are selling a tech product, baking cupcakes or selling a service – what is the value of the market? What is the size of the prize? Is the market too saturated for your business idea? Is there too much competition at different price points for you to make an impact? It's important to research this well. Whilst you do not need to disappear down a rabbit hole of data, you do need to satisfy yourself that your business idea is valid. If you decide to pitch for investment at a later stage, you will certainly be expected to know these answers. Not only will this enable you to demonstrate credibility, it will prove to potential investors that their money can make a return and there is a gap in the market for your product or business.

Let's consider a quick example of someone who wants to set up their business as a personal trainer, offering a wider solution of nutritional advice. You would need to research how much money is spent in the fitness field. What is the size of the population that take part in fitness? What age ranges or genders currently participate? Is there a drop-off trend in certain genders at certain ages that you want to help prevent? You may consider focusing on a local geography population or, if you are taking your business online, then you may want to consider global statistics. How much money is spent on fitness or gym memberships? What are the current health-related issues that mean a focus on nutrition is also needed? All of these questions will help you to understand not only the potential size of the prize but also what exists in the current market and where there is an opportunity to bring something unique. If you find someone else is already providing a similar service, take time to see what they do differently to you. How will your offering be different maybe on price, quality or service?

It's important not to dismiss this part of the business start-up process. You may be clear that you have a good idea and you are passionate and fixed on your intention. Having the data to back up your thinking is always beneficial and you will undoubtedly find new ideas for your business along the way. You may even identify a future consumer need that isn't catered for.

Market research will tell you the current reality and trends. However, it is more important to scan the horizon for future trends. Whatever industry you are in it is important to consider these questions:

What role is technology playing? How are trends changing? How are educational trends shifting? Is there an opportunity to reach new potential customers during the educational phase? Is there an opportunity for a partnership with another business or organization that would provide a steady income and workload? How might partnerships shift the way you set up your business and allocate your business time? Will partnerships still fulfil your passions for your business? Do the partners you have in mind have values that align with yours and strengthen your brand or do they risk damaging or undermining it?

If the trends in your field are changing quickly, how will you stay ahead of the game and ensure that this is reflected in your offering? You may need to study additional qualifications or become an expert on new trends. How might you build in these changing trends to your business plan so that you can be adaptable? Maybe you need a variety of product or service offering as you see a shift dividing your customers into separate groups. Maybe your local consumers are from a certain ethnic background that requires a more diverse awareness of their needs, habits and customs in order for you to provide alternatives.

As you start to research the possibilities for your business, the opportunities may be endless. They may also be so extensive that you feel overwhelmed with where to begin as the opportunities are everywhere. This is where all the work you have done previously on establishing clarity on your vision and values will help to steer you during this marketing phase. Remember to go back to your intention, vision and values and ensure you're sticking to the journey. There may be new and exciting opportunities but take time to consider whether these will pose a distraction at this stage of your start-up or whether they will enhance and redirect in ways you had not considered. Maybe they are valid avenues for the expansion stage of your business. Make a note of them and come back to them in time. You may find the trends in the marketplace have shifted again by the time you're ready to expand your business.

Reflection 18: Know your market

- Consider your business idea. What industry and market are you operating in?
- Does your business span multiple industries?
- What will be your primary industry focus?
- How big is the market – how many people are in that space as consumers?
- How much money is spent in that market?
- How much money is generated in that market?
- What are the top three trends in that market currently?
- What are some of the innovations in that market?
- Where are the most valuable sources of information for your market?
- What websites, technology and forums does your market use?
- What disruption is happening in your market?

Equally important is knowing your target customer. You may think your product is for everyone; however, you cannot market a product to multiple consumers. Products should be marketed to a specific primary audience. Once successful within this niche, your brand will transition more easily in the expansion phase of its life cycle.

Know your customer

> 'Don't find customers for your products,
> find products for your customers.'
> – Seth Godin

It may seem a little strange to start publicizing your business before it's even up and running. However, you don't simply launch a business without a build-up and preparing the customer. Some entrepreneurs find this a challenge and feel that they need to have the product fully in place and perfect before marketing. The truth is the more anticipation and excitement you can create for your product the more successful the launch is likely to be. Imagine spending all this time and effort on establishing your business only to go live without causing much of an impact.

The chances are you need a revenue stream fairly quickly from your business, unless you are launching your venture as a hobby or side hustle and income is secondary. The sooner you start to talk about your business or product two things happen. First, it becomes more real for you and you are less likely to quit or delay. This sense of commitment builds the more you tell people about your intention. Second, you will start to create momentum around the interest and awareness of your product and be able to start gathering insights, gauge interest and procure feedback.

It is evident that you need a clear marketing plan for your business. Whether your start-up is focused locally or globally, the process will be the same – the outcome will simply have wider reach. The first thing you need to consider is the all-important consumer. Who will be buying or using your product? Do you see your product being sold to large corporate organizations or individuals? Do you see your product starting off with individual sales and scaling to partnerships with larger supply chain avenues as the brand awareness and demand increases?

Before you answer these questions, it's important you know who your consumer is. What is your target market? Do you have a clear view of who will and won't purchase your product? Is your product gender specific? The clearer you are on your consumer the more specific you can be in your marketing strategy and where you invest your time and money in promoting your product or service. What is the age range of your consumer? It's very easy to say this product or business is for everyone; however, it is likely that you will have primary consumers and secondary consumers. You need to focus your marketing on your primary consumers.

Once you have spent some time really drilling down to understand your primary consumer, it is important to know how to reach them. Where do they 'hang out' either physically or in the virtual world? How do they spend their time? What are the priorities in their life? Where do people come together to talk about your product? Maybe this already exists within a forum you have created online. The more clearly you define your primary consumer, the more targeted your marketing and networking will be. This is where you shift from knowing your customer to understanding the market in which you want to operate.

Reflection 19: Know your customer

- Who is your primary customer?
- What are their demographics – age, ethnicity, gender, etc.?
- What information do you know about your consumer in terms of their size and scope in the market your product will be launched in?
- Research the statistics of your primary customer in order to demonstrate the scope of the market – this information will be relevant to any future pitch or marketing review.
- Try to quantify the market and the need for your product.
- Then list your secondary consumers – who else may want your product or service?

Having explored the market and the customer trends more clearly, you may find that some assumptions you previously held have changed. You may have additional insight about your target consumer. If your research challenges your assumptions be ready to adapt your business plan, product or service. Tailoring your product or service rather than rigidly forcing it into a market place that has shifted will reap far more benefit.

Entrepreneurs often struggle to change or adapt their initial idea, product or service after having toiled for so long to bring it to inception. It's important to remember that insight and feedback is gold dust. You wouldn't climb a mountain in warm weather gear and keep pushing forward when it starts to snow or rain and assume everything will be ok. You would change, adapt and be prepared.

It is important to bring all of your insight from market and customer research back into your pitch. Any oversight could make the difference between an investor coming on board or opting out from your business venture. A shrewd investor will certainly be clear on market and consumer trends and will spot an entrepreneur who has overlooked any detail. Even informal discussions with potential clients will soon lead to doubts if they see gaps in your product or market knowledge. Insight and research are therefore critical to having a rounded and informed pitch whether formal or informal.

Just as the climber would research conditions for their journey and have a clear route, they would also be sure to prepare for changing landscapes and have the confidence that they have researched sufficiently to cover all eventualities. Market and customer insight is no different. You should feel confident after researching to tell everyone about the market, the consumer needs and how your product or service addresses their needs or problems. You are ready to pitch.

What is a pitch?

'If you cannot explain it simply, you don't understand it well enough.' – Albert Einstein

Every time you talk about your product, you are effectively pitching. It may just be a conversation with friends, family or those in your network; however, how you describe your product and explain its benefits to your immediate support network will also impact how they understand and describe it to others. Every post, video, vlog, blog, discussion about your product is a pitch to a potential consumer so choose your words wisely!

Pitching can therefore take many forms, both formal and informal. You will no doubt have heard about the idea of an elevator pitch – the concept behind this is to hone your product pitch so well that should you meet a potential client or investor, you can quickly and concisely pitch your product in less than the time it takes to ride an elevator with them, which is often only a minute or two. (Unless you're stopping at every floor in a high rise!) So keep it short.

Some of the reflective work you have already done on values, branding and conscious consumers in the early chapters will come in useful here. Your opportunities to pitch to your consumers can come from a range of interactions from face-to-face meetings, forums, online networks or your business media platforms. Whilst these forums may enable a longer introduction to your business, it is important to remember that the attention span of a passive consumer is probably 30 seconds at best. Within that small window, you have to be able to explain what your product is and build their curiosity sufficiently to retain them for a further period of time.

When you own a business and are passionate about your product, it is quite a challenge to formulate a concise pitch.

The easiest way to do this is a funnel approach where you start by gathering all the key points you want to make and slowly cutting them down into more crisp concise pitch statements. We will try a reflection exercise to help.

Reflection 20: Practise your elevator pitch

- If someone asked, 'What do you do?' write down the first thing that comes to your mind to pitch your business. Don't correct yourself or overthink it as you wouldn't have that time in an elevator! Just write or say it out loud and record it.
- Reflect on your first attempt. What was missing? What key words did you forget? Did your pitch cover your product's unique selling point (USP), your values and vision?
- Go back to your vision and values reflection – did these messages and precise words come out?
- Try writing your pitch more clearly now in no more than 300 words, this time without the pressure of the elevator timing!
- Try to condense your pitch even more – can you use language more effectively to ensure every word counts?
- Once you have perfected it, write it clearly and concisely then practise and try it out with your support groups to get the relevant, objective feedback you need.
- Sometimes consider the problem first, then your product. Humans engage emotionally with a story and solution concept.
- Can you open with a statement such as 'One in three people suffer with x or don't have x' therefore...' and your product or service is the solution.

Once you have your neatly formed short pitch written down, ensure you rehearse it well. This will ensure that whenever you are asked what you do, or are introducing yourself at a networking event, you can be sure to quickly and calmly pull out your pitch to steer the conversation whilst keeping the passionate creative energetic salesperson inside you in check.

There will no doubt also be opportunities where you will have to present a more formal pitch. From when we explored the five stages of business, you will now see that different types of pitch may be required at each stage from seed, start-up and growth right through to expansion. You have clarity on your vision, values and brand, and you have taken time to understand and capture information about your consumer and the market in which you want to operate. You have carefully planned and understood your budgeting and sales forecasts. You therefore already have all the ingredients and information to hand to pull your pitch together. In fact, most of the reflection exercises alone will give you the key information for your content. We will look at how you pull everything together in a final pitch reflection later in this chapter.

What's in it for them?

> 'Price is what you pay. Value is what you get.'
> – Warren Buffet

One of the big mistakes that many entrepreneurs make when pitching is to think of their needs first and 'the sell'. The key to a successful pitch is to hook the audience through curiosity and incentive. You may be in front of a financial institution and the hook for them may be long-term partnerships and the ability to also profit from your business. You may be in front of a significant investor who may invest for philanthropic reasons and they will therefore want to hear about the problems you are solving socially or environmentally. You may want your product stocked with a local retailer – how will your product drive footfall to their store or complement rather than dilute their current range? Think investor first and place this upfront in your pitch.

Let's consider our mountain climb and the guide briefing the climber. They would take time to understand the experience of their group, they may have had informal discussions or data beforehand to understand the climber's motivations, and they would demonstrate their knowledge and experience to put the climbers at ease and provide confidence that they were in safe hands. The guide may also end on a positive inspirational note encouraging the climbers to enjoy the journey. Your pitch is no different. You need to engage the audience, understand their motivations, demonstrate your business awareness and engage with them as potential investors.

The audience's motivation is critical to assess prior to any pitch. Try to find out who will be listening to your pitch and do your research. In the same way that you would research for a job interview and learn about a business, the pitch is no different. Learn about the person you are pitching to. What motivates and inspires them? Are they making emotional decisions on where to invest their money? Is their business aligned to your company values? Is your audience strictly business and will they want to just talk numbers? How can you build connection and trust quickly?

Consider whether this pitch is for a short-term relationship that is more transactional or are you looking for a long-term partnership with your audience? Be sure to prepare your pitch in such a way that you will capture, engage and retain the interest and curiosity of the audience throughout. If you have a limited time to present, don't overrun. Ensure you share everything you need to in that time and leave time for some questions. If investors want to know more, they will give more time and ask more questions so stay concise.

Consider whether you have material you can share with them prior to or after your pitch. Be creative – if you are selling a product, consider sending free samples to their teams a week prior to generate some discussions before your pitch. Maybe your target audience is the family or friends of the investor – why not share your product with them ahead of your pitch? Just like a CV that lands with a recruiter, your pitch has to stand out and your product has to stay in mind before, during and even after the pitch.

Reflection 21: Pre-pitch preparation

With some of these ideas in mind think of one or two people or businesses you aspire to pitch to.

- What more do you need to know about them?
- What do you need to know about their businesses?
- Where could you find this information?
- Who are their networks and do you have common connections?
- What are their values and motivations?
- What are some creative ideas that come to mind right now about how you could create excitement before, during or even after you pitch your product or service?

If you can perfect a short elevator pitch and an investor pitch of no more than 5–10 minutes, you will be equipped to market your product or service at any given opportunity. You need only consider the audience to make a quick tweak to your pitch introduction to quickly tailor it to the situation. Having these staple pitch ideas to hand will ensure you are taking a strong and consistent message to the market about your product and brand. The more consistent the messaging around your product, the clearer the brand becomes in the market place as more and more consumers talk about your product and service. Certain words and phrases start to become synonymous with your brand.

The long game...

> 'Your customer doesn't care how much you know
> until they know how much you care.'
> – Damon Richards

Pitching doesn't always have an immediate sale or investment outcome. Often a pitch can be an opportunity to build trust with potential consumers. Consider how you could provide non-sales focused offerings to your potential consumers and build trust. What can you provide for free that will entice the consumer? How could you demonstrate your skill, product or service and let it sell itself rather than formulating any pitch? How could you educate your potential consumer on the problem that your product will solve – without mentioning your product at this stage?

In a world where consumers have a wide variety of choice at their fingertips and can consume at the click of a button, it becomes increasingly important to build trust to establish long-term relationships or to enter into a market that is well established and disrupt it. When consumers are constantly faced with adverts and notifications on all their media platforms pushing them to purchase, it becomes increasingly important to engage with them and build trust informally and when they are relaxed. Take, for example, the music software that makes recommendations based on your taste or the movie provider that makes recommendations based on previous content. This gentle method of suggestion uses AI to suggest rather than force the consumer. The same approach may be needed as you enter an established market or want to gain traction with your product or service. The hard-sell approach is expiring; consider how your product or service can gain trust and interest. Consider sharing helpful information with potential customers and building trust in you and your brand.

By providing consumers with suggested offerings, rather than forcing a sale, you may get to build trust. When the consumer doesn't feel pressured or sold to, this often leads to a softening in their approach, which enables you to build a relationship that won't just be transactional but potentially transformational. On the simplest level, consider the free food samples at your local supermarket or farmers' market. You are enticed to try for free and enjoy with no commitment. Yet, if you and a million other customers start to add that one item to your trolley each week, going forward the impact can be significant sustainable spend.

If you're selling a food product, consider catering at local events with a simple way for consumers to engage further if they choose to. If your business is service based, consider offering some free content or services that will help the business you want to work with through a particular challenge or problem. If you are a coach, offer some free sessions to build rapport and trust. Maybe your business can provide insights and information to your prospective consumer about trends in the market. Recruitment agencies, for example, may share market insights and salary data from your sector with you on a regular basis. If the business finds this helpful, that recruiter may be front of mind when considering an engagement.

When you're an entrepreneur or a small business owner, your mindset is often fixed on sales and growing your business, it often consumes your life as it's your passion. Every interaction is a potential sale opportunity when you don those entrepreneurial sales tinted glasses. Your motivations may not even be financial, your product may solve social or environmental issues, yet your passion may make an interaction feel like an eco-warrior initiation! Sometimes your potential clients just don't want to be sold to.

Knowing your potential consumer and gauging the mood of your audience is critical to success. You may go into a meeting with an agenda only for a stakeholder to be totally consumed and distracted by another problem. You have two options – reschedule your meeting, which may or may not even be possible for some time or help them through their problem. The latter will help to build a deeper relationship and there may even be an 'in' to your pitch later in the discussion. One thing is for sure, forcing a sale when the audience is elsewhere will not be fruitful. You often have to think on your feet in such situations and flex your approach quickly to consider the long game.

Perfecting the formal pitch

> 'If people like you they will listen to you, but if
> they trust you they will do business with you.'
> – Zig Ziglar

Whilst every interaction you have has the potential to form some level of pitch to the audience, it is important to plan, prepare and hone your more formal pitch ideas. A formal pitch may be needed from the moment you have the seed idea for your business right through to expansion depending on your business model and financing needs.

Let's consider the key information you need to get across to your audience. For the purposes of this exercise we are going to assume this is a pitch for investment. Whilst this content will be relevant for most pitches, be sure to tweak your pitch for the audience based on what we have covered previously in the chapter.

An investor will want to know several key elements from your pitch:

- What do you need from them?
- What is the problem?
- What is the solution?
- What is the size of the market for this solution?
- What is your product?
- What are the financials in terms of cost to produce, sales projections and scalability?
- What are the other consumer options / competition and why is your product better?

Below is an example, followed by a reflection for you to start capturing information for your pitch. Remember to look back at your previous reflections to use the same messaging, wording and branding when pitching your product or service.

Now let's try working on your pitch outline.

Example

What do you need from them? I am looking for a $50k investment for a 10% share in my company.

What is the problem? One in three people will suffer with their mental health.

What is the solution? My application will track and notify the user of potential mental health decline and ensure immediate access to medical professionals to offer support and advice and help diagnose early symptoms of health problems.

What is the size of the market for this solution? With over 250 million impacted by mental health worldwide, the market size is significant and continues to grow.

What is your product? My app is free to download and compatible with all smartphones and involves some basic set-up data and ongoing engagement with the app.

What are the financials in terms of cost to produce, sales projections and scalability? The app has already been produced and simply requires exclusive partnership deals with relevant healthcare providers in order to become the global tool for supporting mental health.

What are the other consumer options / competition and why is your product better? My app has been endorsed by, and I have confirmed partnerships in place with, the top healthcare providers across four major continents so far, which no other app has managed to secure. I am looking for investment to expand this coverage across more markets.

You will also need to be prepared to answer questions from potential investors so, whilst your pitch should be short and concise, take time to consider what questions an investor may have. Who are the competition? What is different about your product? How does it compare to the competition product? Is the pricing higher because it has a unique quality? The more prepared you are with potential answers the smoother the pitch will be.

Again, practise your pitch with different stakeholders across your support group and ask them to pose questions – the more challenging the question the better prepared you can be with a response. There are only so many questions an investor or potential client might ask. The more practice you have, the broader your stakeholder questions, the more likely you will be to have answers for all the questions you may come across, which will give your more confidence for your pitch.

Reflection 22: Perfecting your pitch

- What do you need from the audience?
- What is the problem?
- What is the solution?
- What is the size of the market for this solution?
- What is your product?
- What are the financials in terms of cost to produce, sales projections and scalability?
- What are the other consumer options / competition and why is your product better?

Once you have perfected your pitch, try rehearsing in front of your support groups. A perfect pitch on paper is no use if that's where it stays and you certainly don't want to be presenting it for the first time in a live scenario! Ask your practice audience to ask challenging questions and provide feedback to you on your response and delivery. Remember to use the correct people from your support group for this exercise. This is the time to use those direct, honest, supportive and objective contacts who will help to enhance your pitch and challenge you. This is not the time to use your best friend who always says the right thing and tells you it's perfect!

Once you have rehearsed your pitch, use your local forums and online networks to practise until you are comfortable with the pitch.

Your investors will know the market inside out so be sure to get your facts clear using the latest reference points. Always remember, no matter how intimidating it may seem, no one knows your business better than you and, there are only so many questions that investors will want to ask. In the same way that you can anticipate and prepare for 99% of interview questions, a pitch is no different. Equally, as with an interview, if you don't know the answer it's much better to be honest than to deceive someone you want to invest in your career or business.

Above all else, remember that most successful entrepreneurs, are told 'No' 99 times before they get a yes. Remember to prepare yourself mentally for the pitch. How will you deal with the potential outcome? Have your post-pitch plan in place whether that is celebrating success or reflecting on failure. The previous reflections in the book will have set you up to manage either outcome so be sure to use them as part of your pitch preparation.

Remember that sometimes no may actually mean not just yet, not today or not with the current offering in its present shape or form. A no doesn't always means the door is closed. Listen to feedback from investors carefully. They may be offering golden advice to help you succeed next time or to tweak your idea for the future. We will look at how you can plan for success and manage setbacks and 'failures' in the next chapter.

7

Success, setbacks and 'failures'

How can I plan for uncertainty?

Success: what are my measures of success?

'The road to success and the road to failure
are almost exactly the same.' – Colin R. Davis

In Chapter 2, we explored your motivation for starting a business and identifying your true purpose. You reflected on whether your goals were intrinsic and philanthropic or extrinsic and materialistic. Purpose is very much a personal driver; however, we reflected on ensuring that you were motivated for the right reasons and considered how to dig beneath material goals for more purposeful motivations. So, why are those reflections important now? Once your business is up and running, your purpose and goals will determine your vision of what success looks like.

You may have set out with a simple goal of climbing this mountain. You will have milestones along the way – reaching certain altitudes or famous points in the climb that others have reached before you. Then you summit. Is that the end goal alone to reach the top? Or, is there a little more to that goal? Are you actually climbing for charity, or in memory of someone? Is there more to the purpose than just reaching the top? Maybe it is symbolic of having reached a certain level of fitness or having overcome an illness? The same may be true of setting up your business. Once you have reached the day of go live – is that it? Or is there something much deeper or broader that this journey has stood for? It may just be the beginning and success is still further ahead and based on sales, popularity and customer behaviour? It is important to reflect on what success means to you on this journey and be sure to know that it need not be limited to one event. Many milestones are worthy of success and it's important to celebrate them all. Reflect continually on the climb to date; look back at the view in awe and celebration. Look forward to the future goals too and celebrate them as they rise rather than rushing past them all as you head to the next summit.

Why not start by practising a little reflection on your success so far? Take time to reflect on how far you have come through this book and what an achievement it is to have reached this point. Before you started this book, you may have had little more than a seed. By now, you should have some great ideas, plans and some structure to how you will make this seed a success, no matter how big or small.

Having come this far and taken time to plan your approach alongside reflection and balancing other commitments, you should feel better prepared and more confident that you are able to overcome the challenges that lie ahead. Your mindset will be better prepared to notice barriers when they arise and realize that they may be necessary to redirect you towards a better path. When barriers do arise, be sure to come back to your reflections and remind yourself how you decided to approach and overcome these barriers.

Starting your own business is a huge goal in itself. However, as you near the launch of your business, those measures of success become your guiding focus. How will you measure that you are on the right path and doing everything you set out to do? It's important to consider those moonshot goals from earlier in the book and also to set your milestones goals for getting there. Why did you set up this business? What were some of the values you put in place?

We discussed purpose over profit very early on and, whilst your business will hopefully generate a revenue that works for you, your success may actually be measured by far more intrinsic goals. Aside from financial results, you may be motivated by how much you are giving back into other areas such as charity or how your business is helping to drive sustainability. Undoubtedly, the more profitable your business, the more other organizations will benefit from your proceeds; however, you may be motivated by the latter rather than the former and the intrinsic reward of seeing your impact.

If you are measuring your success by contribution rather than profit, this is a much more philanthropic approach and may just align more with your consumer. This consumer loyalty and awareness of your sustainable and charitable profit share will, in fact, increase consumer spend. Setting business targets and goals around your profit share can be far more rewarding than profit-based goals alone. There is an increasing trend towards start-ups donating proceeds to charitable causes or driving the focus of product sustainability. In a world where conscious consumerism is on the rise, starting a business without these tie-ins creates immediate business disadvantage. Be sure to consider creating connections to relevant causes with values aligned to yours and those of your consumer.

This model of connectivity to a cause may not seem as feasible in a service-driven business; however, your goals may still be intrinsically driven. If you are offering health and nutrition solutions, your measure of success may be seeing how people's lifestyle and wellbeing improves. If your business offers training or coaching solutions, you could always consider offering a percentage of your profits to educational charities or organizations that would resonate with your clients. If your client base is large and diverse, you need not overcomplicate synchronicity – most people simply value the fact that there is a connected cause or charity benefiting from their partnership with you.

If you are creating a significant tech innovation or idea, it may be that you simply need one sale to a big tech giant; however, your product may benefit the lives of millions of people through connection or simplification. Your success may be measured by consumption – seeing your app utilized as a core tool in the market. If you have set up a small local business, maybe your success is based on achieving local recognition or becoming the 'go-to' place in your town for that product. Whatever your measures of success, ensure they are clear, documented and frequently reviewed to measure your progress. If these success measures are your north star on this climb, then making sure you are on the right path will be your confirmation that you are heading in the right direction.

Clarifying these measures of success and goals is a great way to see that you are fulfilling your ambitions as set out from the start. These goals may evolve as your business grows. The key is to acknowledge the difference that recognition plays over reward in terms of its intrinsic value. Purpose over profit and starting a business to add value or make a difference, are the more meaningful measures of success.

Reflection 23: Measures of success

- What did you define as your goals earlier in the book? Were they extrinsic or intrinsic?
- What measure will validate those goals being achieved?
- What are the milestone measures of success along the way?

- What are your tangible measures, e.g. sales, income, profit?
- What are your non-financial measures, e.g. customer following, repute customers, referrals?
- What are your sustainability measures, e.g. percentage of recycled products, carbon neutral efficiency, profit share to charitable organizations?
- What are the rewards or recognition you aspired to – world number one? Top ten local provider? Professional body award recognition?

We also touched upon entrepreneurs who may be setting up their business for fun or as a hobby. You may have set up your business to prove to yourself that you can! This alone is a worthwhile journey and milestone. Simply getting to the point of opening a business and showcasing your work is enough for many people. What happens next for them is a bonus, the journey has been the reward. In the same way, an author may be satisfied that selling one book that helps one reader to make a difference to their life is sufficient a reward for their effort. Anything more is a bonus.

Success clearly isn't just about the numbers – it can be based on impact, feedback, sustainability and contribution to the broader environment. When you considered your why, your purpose, early on in the book, these were some of the key underlying drivers that started you on this journey. Wanting to make a difference, impacting people's lives and enabling them through your business, product or service was the starting point. Remember that aha moment? Never forget that seed, the idea that started the journey.

Yes, your service is not free and you may need to make a living in order to sustain this business; however, the motivation and drive to do the right thing can far offset the financial gains. Your consumers will buy into these values and stay loyal to your brand as a result. Purpose over profit and focusing on being valuable not successful will, in turn, make your business the most profitable and successful it can be.

Setbacks and 'failures': how will I navigate obstacles?

'If you are not failing you are not innovating.'
– Elon Musk

The journey of an entrepreneur is one of continuous discovery and learning. If you speak to successful entrepreneurs, they have often had numerous setbacks before becoming what they describe as successful. The key to dealing with your journey is based upon mindset. We have spent quite some time on this throughout the book.

Each 'failed' business that an entrepreneur has is, more often than not, described by them as a necessary learning that made their latest venture successful. The mindset of an entrepreneur is one that accepts setbacks as redirection and learning. However, most entrepreneurs only accept this in hindsight. The essence of this book is for you to prepare yourself with this approach with foresight.

Having a healthy mindset that allows you to accept setbacks and let go of them quickly will enable you to fast track your ability to progress. The more time spent becoming angry, frustrated or dismayed when things don't go as planned, is simply delaying your ability to move forward and impacting your mindset in such a way that a creative solution moves further away.

If you recall very early on in the book, we talked about positive affirmations and how to shift your doubts into positive statements. The same is true of setbacks. Throughout this book, you will have practised turning adversity into possibility through the various exercises and reflections, as well as building in routines to your day to help you switch off. You have the tools to turn setbacks into questions. What is this teaching me? What have I learned from this experience that I can reshape to take forwards in any business venture?

Many business books and articles on entrepreneurship will talk about resilience. In business you need to be resilient and keep pushing forwards, keep fighting against adversity and keep moving on. Whilst in some respects this may be true, it's also important to know when this doesn't add value longer term.

If we consider our mountain climb analogy, there will be times when you need to literally weather the storm and come out the other side of your journey and for that you need to push through the temporary challenges. There will be times, however, when you need to see that resilience is not the right option. If weather comes that will impact your climb, if it becomes life-threatening or the risk of rescue or survival is surpassed, this level of resilience only has one outcome and it isn't a positive one for the climber.

Even the most experienced of climbers will know when to stop. We are often taught not to quit, to keep pushing, to find a way, yet sometimes knowing when to quit in business is the smarter move. With too much resilience in business, you will fail to recognize when a business is beyond recovery and keep driving forward, losing money and failing your customers in the hope that something will come and save the business.

With too little resilience, you may stop at the first sign of a setback or a dip in sales and consider it time to wrap up and quit whilst you're ahead. Low levels of resilience may result in you dismissing your venture as having worked well whilst it lasted. This level of resilience is akin to the mountain climber who turns back in the first storm – often to find that glorious sunshine follows. Some may even give up and not even take time to look back as they have already abandoned the mountain climb goal altogether.

So how do you find the right level of resilience and know when to call it a day or keep pushing forwards? We talked early on in the book about constantly scanning the horizon for new trends and technologies and also understanding consumer trends and being able to pre-empt these. You will have set time aside to continually build reflection and horizon scanning into your business plan and model in order to join the dots on what the future of your business or industry holds. Granted, you cannot pre-empt every scenario yet, even global incidents such as the pandemic had been foreseen. The only question unknown was when.

There will be times when scanning the horizon allows you to shift your business model and pivot in order to stay relevant. Take the classic examples of the past – businesses that used to rent movies were not quick enough to see a shift to online streaming and the birth of Netflix. There are many examples where industries or business missed the opportunity to pivot.

We saw the shift towards digital and the evolution of smartphones resulting in the downturn of camera technology and businesses such as Kodak were severely impacted. Music stores died when online streaming was born. Online streaming even evolved quickly from a pay-per-song download with iTunes to Spotify subscription to an infinite catalogue that even uses AI to inform you what songs you may want to listen to.

Technology and AI is impacting the dynamic of many businesses and we will see more of this in the next few years. If you are starting a business in 2021, by 2025 it will surely be very different as a result of technology and may even become irrelevant by 2030.

Adaptability over resilience

'The secret of change is to focus all of your energy,
not on fighting the old, but on building the new.'
– Dan Millman

The ability of big brands to stay relevant and extend their shelf life is increasingly dependent upon their ability to adapt rather than to be resilient. We explored some examples of this in Chapter 2 where businesses changed their entire model or even product offering when faced by a pandemic. Changing and flexing with shifting trends; development new technologies; experimenting with new ideas alongside current methodologies are replacing the concept of business resilience. Adaptability is the new resilience of the business world.

As an entrepreneur, it's important to develop adaptability into your business model. It also very much relies on you, as the business owner, to have an adaptable mindset and approach. The tools and reflections to date will have helped to introduce these ideas; however, they need to be continually applied and practised in order to become second nature. The more that you practise the steps within this book and take time to build them into your routine, the sooner they will become an almost natural response and way of operating.

If your business is expanding to the point where you will be hiring other people into your business, you also need to hire individuals with an adaptability mindset. Hire the creative people, the thinkers and dreamers; particularly if this is something you are struggling to adapt to yourself. Hiring your weaknesses can be the best decision you will make. It could just end up saving your business at a critical juncture.

It is important to remain adaptable as a proactive trait not simply a reaction to threat. Ensuring that your business is proactive and not reactive will place you on the front foot when change arises. Your consumer will also notice this. Consumers want to be the first to try new things, to see something new and experiment too. When your consumer sees that you are proactive and adaptable to new ideas, technologies and trends, they are more likely to stay engaged and interested in your brand.

Adaptability may even be core to your brand and values. If this is the heart of your business, then you certainly need to be going first, experimenting and taking risks to try new things. This doesn't necessarily mean abandoning the current ways. It can be that your current model continues but you introduce new and different options to test consumer appetite.

When you are simply reactive in your approach, you become a 'me too' player. For example, introducing a new product flavour because everyone else seems to be doing it may not add any value. Remember to stay focused on what the customer wants, not solely what competitors are doing and you are copying. The moment you start operating in this reactive space and looking to your competitors, you are missing the big shift on the horizon.

Consider the concept of meat-free products. We are seeing a shift towards sustainability and an increase in veganism across the globe to the point where the large fast food chains are not moving against these shifts but embracing them alongside their model. Large food chains see that consumer trends are slowly moving away from their core product – meat.

If large food chains were to focus on resilience and weathering the vegan storm, it is likely they would diminish over time. Big food chains are, however, learning from the failures of past businesses and adopting a partnership approach, providing the consumer with both options. There will, no doubt, come a tipping point where the vegan and conscious consumer movement will outweigh the non-vegan movement.

Currently, the large food chains are supporting the shift to meat-free consumption; however, there will come a tipping point whereby the consumer opts to shop from a chain whose ethics are purer than one that simply provides both options to the consumer. The brand with no conflict between plant-based and animal-based food products will no doubt win the conscious consumer war in time.

So, it is evident that setbacks can, in fact, be flags to your business to redirect, to adapt and to innovate a new way forward. They are not signs to hold firm and be resilient. Setbacks and challenges are an indication of the need to shift. When you need to shift your approach, you need to shift your mindset and this is where the tools and reflections from earlier in the book will help you to reposition and reframe your approach.

There may also be times in your business venture when you need to recognize that resilience is not the answer and adaptability may not be an option. Even when you can see the horizon and join the dots, you may not have the means financially or physically to make a shift or make the shift in time. It is equally important in business to know when to walk away. That does not mean to say you have failed. It can simply be a build-up of circumstances that mean, despite adaptability and creativity, you are simply unable to weather the change. Large chains can often come in and simply undercut your model on price, service a broader consumer in terms of reach and leverage economies of supply chains that allow growth you cannot compete with.

Does this mean you have failed? Or, have you learned something about business that you would not have gained without this experience. Maybe this experience will feed into a new business idea that is highly successful and has an edge over large business because of this very experience. Again, it's all about mindset. What will you tell yourself if it comes to the point where your current business has to cease?

This will no doubt be your biggest reflection and you can spend it focusing on all the things that should have been or you can focus on all the things that went well and that you learned. If you can control your mindset and approach you will come to see there is no such thing as failure only growth. If many of the inventors of our time had quit rather than learn we may be living in a very different world today.

Framing setbacks: internal v external

**'Exceptional people turn life setbacks into
future successes' – Carol S. Dweck**

Setbacks do not necessarily mean the end of the road and, in fact, they may just be the beginning of something new for your business. If you are still the sole person driving the business and working alone, it may be the right time to go back to your business plan and reflect.

What was your original goal and the values you set out for your business? Is this setback internal and personal? It may be something such as focus, energy or conflict. We have many events that happen in our lives that can shift our path and shift our perspective. It is important to reflect when these events happen.

The reflections and exercises throughout this book are not only focusing on the horizon and the external but very much the internal shifts and challenges that you may face. If this challenge or setback is internal consider your support networks that we explored in the reflection exercise in Chapter 4. Who were those people you identified as sounding boards for your journey? Which type of support do you need right now? Is it the sympathetic ear from a friend or family member? Is it the objective voice of experience from your mentor? Maybe you need both but in sequential order?

Setbacks are merely change curves and you need to figure out what support you need at each stage of that curve to get you out the other side. You already have the framework and the map to know where to turn. You need to decide what you need now and what will help you most today with a clear view on what you need to help you move forwards tomorrow.

Your support network was established for this very purpose so it's important to utilize it. No doubt you will have been using that network almost subconsciously through the less complex quandaries of business and the emotional journey. When the setback appears more significant or complex, your approach to resolve it needs to be more structured and intentional.

If your setback is a lack of creativity and not seeing the woods for the trees, find that support mechanism that allows you to switch off. It may be exercise with a friend or taking time to do some yoga or meditation and putting the problem away for another day. We explored how the answers often come when you are performing mundane tasks or thinking of something totally different. The switch between left and right brain activity can be sufficient enough to bring the solution. Your brain is a very complex but smart computer and sometimes it simply needs a reboot.

Take time to reflect on why you started. Is the passion still there when you reflect back on your goals and values? If the passion has subsided, is discipline enough to keep you moving forward or do you simply need a break? Sometimes doing nothing can be the best way to find answers and new solutions.

If you find that your mindset is consumed by a setback or the task ahead, take time to reflect on the journey so far. Consider capturing all the things you have learnt in the last 12 months and actually write them down. You will be amazed at what you have learned. We spend our lives so caught up in moving forward and constant change that we sometimes forget to look how far we have come or even just spend some time being present. Only the now is real, the past is gone and the future hasn't happened yet. Become present and practise putting your setback into perspective.

If your setback is external, go back to your reflections and consider whether you had already captured and foreseen a possible solution. Your initial reflection on the horizon scanning exercises may have actually foreseen this shift and you have become so focused on the day-to-day that you simply forgot to look up and ensure you were adapting. What support do you need for external calibration? You have identified who can support with emotional or physical setbacks. It is now time to consider your professional support network.

Do you have mentors in place who may have experience of dealing with setbacks? Do you have a well-established forum or group either locally or virtually where you can sense check your journey or use the group as a sounding board? Be open to all avenues of support. You may be surprised where solutions come from. A mentor or forum member in a totally different field of expertise may just ask the right question of you that will fire up a new line of thinking.

If you hit a real block and feel there is nowhere to turn within your network, consider paying for an external coaching session. The great thing about a coach is they do not need to have any experience in your field; they simply guide you to change your thinking through the coaching and questioning process. A good coach will be able to challenge your current thinking pattern and help you to break out from a loop or pattern in which you are unable to work towards a solution. If you don't have any setbacks currently it can be worth completing this exercise in readiness for managing setbacks when they arise.

Reflection 24: Recalibrating

- Is your setback internal or external?
- What is driving your current setback?
- What is within your control and what is out of your control? If something is out of your control either look for an alternative or address your response to it as you practised in Reflection 9.
- Is there one issue or a range of issues that each need addressing?
- Who in your support groups are the best resource to help address each concern?
- Which of your support groups can help you switch off from the problems altogether for some time to allow you to rest, reset and stop to take a mountain view?
- What can you do alone that you know will make you feel better immediately if your support networks are not accessible?
- What is within your control that can be adjusted to ease the setback pressure, e.g. can you extend a timeline, push back meetings, etc. to give you space?

For theoretical examples:

- Categorize your potential support solutions for internal setbacks and external setbacks.
- Identify what actions you can take that you know help you to switch off. It could be exercise, or time with certain people, or taking a drive to a certain location – note down what works for you to give you perspective.
- Be clear on your framework and steps to manage setbacks using the above reflections.

Avoiding stress and burnout

'We live under the delusion that burnout is the price
we have to pay for success, which is untrue.'
– Arianna Huffington

The concepts of stress and burnout have been around for a few decades and, fortunately are being more widely recognized and discussed both socially and in the workplace. The concepts of self-care and wellbeing are very much the antidote to stress and burnout, yet the degree to which these are seen as socially accepted and encouraged varies greatly.

In the corporate world, stress and burnout have long been acknowledged as having a presence and are often perceived as an unavoidable side effect of working in certain industries or sectors. There is still some way to go to overcome this; however, on an individual level, awareness of the importance of health and wellbeing is on the rise. Increasingly, more and more people are tuning in to the various methods that provide an outlet for managing stress and burnout.

The global pandemic in 2020 was a significant turning point that highlighted the importance of health and social connections above all things material. The pandemic placed a spotlight on wellbeing like never before. The forced restriction of social human connectivity was a global phenomenon and, whilst virtual methods of connection could be leveraged, the impact of prolonged physical and social human disconnection was evident.

As an entrepreneur, the journey can be a lonely one. We have explored how to leverage support groups effectively, and it is also important to identify triggers for when you need support before it's too late. Understanding what stress and burnout mean to you is critical in ensuring you can take remedial action before they take over. If you can identify stress factors, then you can certainly ensure you take the steps needed to avoid burnout.

Let us first explore what we mean by the concepts of stress and burnout. Stress is often a mental response to a situation that also produces physical symptoms. It is hardwired into the human DNA to support our fight or flight response. Stress can therefore be a positive and necessary part of the human function; however, too much stress or prolonged stress, can be harmful.

Stress causes chemical changes in the body that manifest in physical responses such as increased heart rate, blood pressure and a change in breathing patterns. These responses were important for preparing the body to perform when faced by threats when humans had to co-exist in the wild with animals that posed a threat. Stress would prepare the body to fight or flee a situation.

In the same way today, a level of stress can help humans to perform and meet deadlines or focus to work efficiently. These short sharp bursts of stress allow performance in the moment to certain situations or stimuli. What enables the body to respond successfully to intermittent stress or peaks required for performance, however, are the prolonged periods in-between where the body operates in a state of calm. The body needs to spend more time in this state in order to perform effectively in those moments of flight or fight.

When these periods of stress are prolonged this can lead to burnout. The human body is not designed to operate in a state of stress for prolonged periods. The physical impact of prolonged stress can result in more serious long-term impact on the ability of the body and mind to recover and can result in burnout.

Some of the warning signs of stress can start as seemingly small and sporadic events so it is important to notice when they occur. Typical triggers may include being irritable, demotivated, not sleeping and withdrawing from social events with family and friends. Recognizing these early warning signs is important. These small triggers can turn into embedded patterns of behaviour resulting in negative patters of thought resulting in prolonged periods of pessimism. The longer these patterns continue the more likely they are to lead to burnout where individuals experience a loss of motivation, a decline in self-care and an inability to change patterns of thought in order to move forwards. At this stage many people also experience physical symptoms such as headaches, lethargy and digestive problems to name but a few.

Clearly, stress and burnout are definitely states that we all should avoid; however, sometimes this is easier said than done. For an entrepreneur, it can be hard not to fall into the trap of operating in a permanent state of stress and readiness for fight or flight. Most entrepreneurs are creative, active and high-energy individuals who, by nature, are therefore more prone to operating on the edge of stress for prolonged periods of time. If you are the sole person managing your business, there is no team to share the workload.

The key for entrepreneurs to avoid stress and burnout is to build wellbeing into their plan from the beginning. Throughout the book, the reflection exercises have prepared you to manage this approach and to build this into your journey. The key is to ensure you utilize it.

As we explored in the early chapters, your best ideas may just come in moments of reflection. When you stop to take the mountain view rather than the trail view, you can gain perspective. Stress and burnout are firmly embedded in the trail journey, noticing their presence and avoiding them can only be achieved when you have built reflection and downtime into the journey.

We explored the concepts of physical exercise, mindfulness, yoga and meditation early on. These should now be firmly embedded in your mind as elements that do not distract from your goal and your path but are very much activities that will bring clarity and focus and enhance your entrepreneurial journey. You have also explored how to manage your time effectively to build these activities in or combine them with your journey so that the two are strongly intertwined.

Self-care, switching off and socializing with your support groups and friends will always enhance your perspective and performance. The more we isolate, operate for prolonged periods of stress and sacrifice sleep for perceived progress, the further you will move away from the best version of you and your business. Success at all costs is not the purpose of this journey. Success through a healthy, mindful and balanced approach to entrepreneurship is the desired and achievable goal. When problems and challenges arise you need only turn to your reflections, support groups and wellness practices to find your way forward.

Diversify solutions

'We cannot solve our problems with the same thinking we used when we created them.' – Albert Einstein

We all experience the world from a different perspective. What you may see as a setback, someone else will see as a great opportunity. What you find easy to overcome, others would see as a significant challenge. The beauty of such a diverse range of perspectives is that the broader your network the more you can tap into this diversity of thinking and engage with people who will challenge your own approach. These perspectives are an amalgamation of your thoughts, experiences, upbringing, education, religion and so many other socio-political factors. No two people are the same. Whilst we tend to gravitate towards like-minded people, it is likely you will hold differing views on certain topics; however, your common beliefs outweigh the differences.

This uniformity of thinking may not be helpful when you experience setbacks. When you look at your support network it is likely you will find more uniformity than divergence. Think about where you can go for different perspectives. Challenge yourself to go to the people who don't think like you and get their perspective on your current perceived setback. This may be a difficult option to pursue but be prepared to listen to opposing views. After all, your own views have brought you to a dead end.

One thing is for certain, setbacks are temporary. In their worst form, they may be finite for your business venture – the experience and the situation are still temporary. If you have to declare bankruptcy, you will still move on from that position. Many successful entrepreneurs have been bankrupt throughout their journeys to success. Many bestselling authors have been rejected a million times before becoming successful; even scientists with lifesaving or life-changing ideas have been ignored or ridiculed. Without those experiences, their most successful business and ideas may have failed or worse, never been realized.

This brings us to the concept of perspective and gratitude. You may have explored these through your reflections and the journey through mindfulness and meditation. Being able to maintain perspective and gratitude can go a long way to helping you maintain clarity throughout the setback process and through the good times too.

Gratitude and perspective

'Be thankful for what you have; you'll end up having more. If you concentrate on what you don't have, you will never, ever have enough.' – Oprah Winfrey

We have all had those moments where we are wallowing in self-pity and a friend comes in with a statement to put our minuscule suffering into perspective compared to matters in the wider world. This idea of perspective and gratitude actually starts at a young age as our parents try to teach these concepts. When we complain as children that we are bored yet we have more toys and forms of entertainment at our hands than many children in other countries. Or when our parents tell us to eat our food as there are starving children in the world.

Perspective is a key building block to mental wellbeing and developing a mindset of gratitude. When we are able to develop gratitude and perspective with our inner voice rather than that of our parents, we are able to form habits and patterns around gratitude and perspective that become almost subconscious reactions to adversity.

You can train your mind to put setbacks into perspective. You can practise gratitude to stay focused on what you have rather than what exists outside of you or your reach. In the first world we have become so used to everything being accessible whether that's food, electricity, running water or Wi-Fi. Take note of how your mind responds when those things are removed or impacted, even if only temporarily.

If you are without hot water for a day, are you consumed with anger at what you don't have or, do you change your perspective to one that remembers you at least have running water, which millions of people are without. When you are unable to access Wi-Fi, do you see this as an opportunity to disconnect and be present or do you spend time feeling angry that you may be missing out on everyone's virtual life when, in reality, you are simply missing your own pass by in front of you. This simple shift in perspective from the inner voice can make a huge difference to how you approach life day in day out and also how you approach business setbacks.

Being aware of your inner voice, your response and your ability to reframe that inner voice to respond in a more positive or balanced way will help you to transition more quickly through perceived setbacks. You may find with a little perspective they aren't even setbacks at all!

When your supplier fails to deliver, you can spend your time getting angry or you can see this as an opportunity to test those back up plans and secondary supplier plans you put into place in Chapter 5 when you looked at business continuity planning. You may find this secondary supplier opens your eyes to a new supplier model altogether that you wouldn't have considered without this 'setback'.

If you are providing a service face-to-face and a pandemic hits, you can decide to cease your business and quit or see the opportunity to shift your business into a virtual forum that actually has global reach and does not require travel and limited attendance.

At this point in your journey there will no doubt have been a shift in what you see as your true values, your 'why' and measures of success. Before starting this journey, success may have looked very different for you; maybe the outcome remains the same but the path and the journey have altered. Being an entrepreneur need not go hand in hand with burnout. Many entrepreneurs become an 'overnight' success after several attempts at a business venture. Ensure you maintain a balanced mindset, use the tools and techniques throughout this book and prioritize your wellbeing. In doing so you will have learned that you are able to change your perspective, by practising gratitude you can awaken to the opportunities in every scenario.

Throughout this journey, the focus has been not only to start your business and bring your idea to life but to do so without burning out. Through discipline and focus you can integrate health and wellbeing into the excitement and chaos of venturing into the unknown. As we come to the end of this chapter we approach the beginning of your journey. You have reached the summit and the destination stretches out in front of you once again. There will be so many new and exciting challenges and opportunities ahead as you choose to start your next mountain climb into entrepreneurship. Ignite the spark for the new challenge, bring your business idea to life, do not let your ideas die and remember:

'Be grateful for all the closed doors, detours and road blocks that prevented you from paths and places not meant for you and lead you to something better.'
– Unknown

Your journey begins now…

Conclusion

Having progressed through this book, you will no doubt have a different perspective on the entrepreneurial journey that lies ahead of you from when you embarked. It is now time to bring your ideas into reality. If you have completed the reflections in the online tool on the author website, you will also have a handy referral document, that will enable you to quickly return to the key thoughts and reflections on critical topics.

If your journey is a slow steady climb, the reflection tool is a great way to refresh without having to revisit entire topics or start over on your plan. If you can set aside time to read this book, you have demonstrated that you can certainly carve out time to progress your business idea through to reality. Through small habits every day, week or month, your business idea can come to life. Building habits around your business is the first step in moving your idea forward.

The journey need not be one of stress and burnout. Through small habits of mindfulness and a focus on health and wellbeing as an integral part of your journey, the path to establishing your business can be one of balance, growth, fun and even adventure! If you embed your affirmations and maintain a healthy perspective, you will experience the entire journey as one of growth and evolution. If you are learning there is no failure or disadvantage.

The time it takes to bring your idea into reality is in your hands. The journey can be as fast or as steady as you decide. You set the pace, you are in control and, when external factors arise, you are also equipped with tools to help you respond not react to the environment. Stepping back, slowing down, and taking a break can all be equally productive in helping you move forwards.

This book is your guide. The journey has only just begun and you can revisit chapters and reflections of your journey to reinforce the learning. If you feel overwhelmed, you can revisit the relevant reflections and chapters to refocus and realign. The reflection tool is organic and, as you and your business ideas evolve and change, you can utilize the tool not only to update your current plan but who knows, you may even start a whole new business.

Now that you have reached this summit, look out onto the horizon and set your eyes firmly on what new challenges lie ahead. It is time to bring your idea into reality and ignite that spark.